Jazz, Funk & Soul Classics for Ukulele

WISE PUBLICATIONS
part of The Music Sales Group
London / New York / Paris / Sydney / Copenhagen / Berlin / Madrid / Hong Kong / Tokyo

Published by
Wise Publications
14-15 Berners Street, London W1T 3LJ, UK.

Exclusive Distributors:
Music Sales Limited
Distribution Centre, Newmarket Road, Bury St Edmunds, Suffolk IP33 3YB, UK.
Music Sales Pty Limited
Units 3-4, 17 Willfox Street, Condell Park, NSW 2200, Australia.

Order No. AM1009041
ISBN: 978-1-78305-598-2

Compiled and edited by Adrian Hopkins.
Music arranged by Matt Cowe.
Music processed by Paul Ewers Music Design.
Cover designed by Tim Field.
Cover images courtesy of Fotolia.

Printed in the EU.

Your Guarantee of Quality:

As publishers, we strive to produce every book
to the highest commercial standards.

This book has been carefully designed to minimise
awkward page turns and to make playing from it a real pleasure.

Particular care has been given to specifying acid-free, neutral-sized paper
made from pulps which have not been elemental chlorine bleached.
This pulp is from farmed sustainable forests and was produced
with special regard for the environment.

Throughout, the printing and binding have been planned to ensure a sturdy,
attractive publication which should give years of enjoyment.

If your copy fails to meet our high standards,
please inform us and we will gladly replace it.

www.musicsales.com

Ukulele tablature explained

A few songs in this collection feature ukulele tab. Tablature graphically represents the ukulele fingerboard. Each horizontal line represents a string (GCEA), and each number represents a fret. The top line of the tab is the A string (the one that's closest to the floor when you're playing); the line below that is the E string; the line below that is the C string and the bottom line of the tab is the G string.

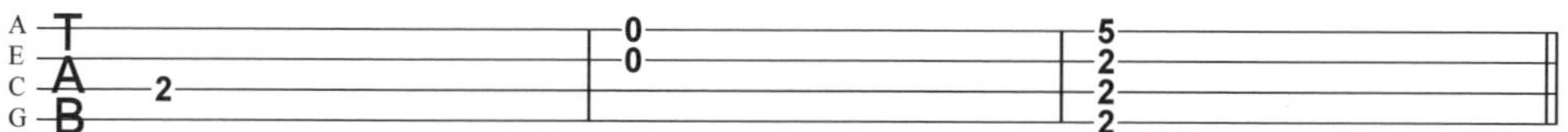

The numbers that appear on the tab indicate which string to play and what fret to play it at. In the first bar above, the 2nd fret on the C string should be played (the note D). In the second bar, the two top strings (E and A) should be played. The third bar shows a D chord, and all four strings should be played.

Definitions for special ukulele notation

HAMMER-ON: Strike the first note with one finger, then sound the second note (on the same string) with another finger by fretting it without picking.

PULL-OFF: Place both fingers on the note to be sounded, strike the first note and without picking, pull the finger off to sound the second note.

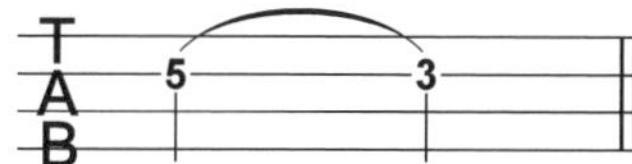

LEGATO SLIDE (GLISS): Strike the first note and then slide the same fret-hand finger up or down to the second note. The second note is not struck.

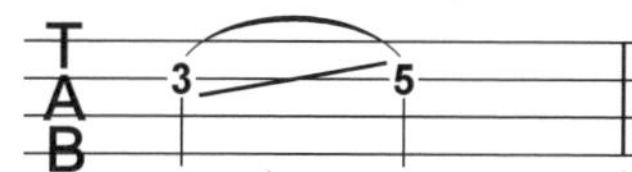

Additional musical definitions

Repeat bars between signs.

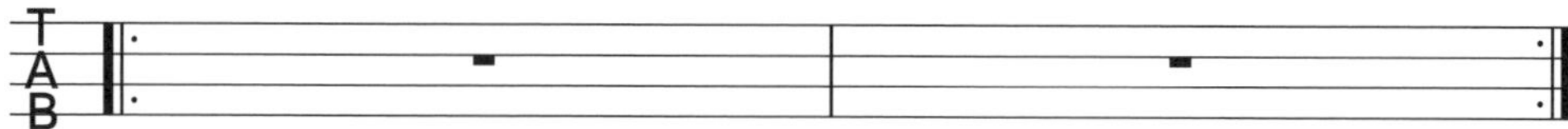

When a repeat section has different endings, play the first ending only the first time and the second ending only the second time.

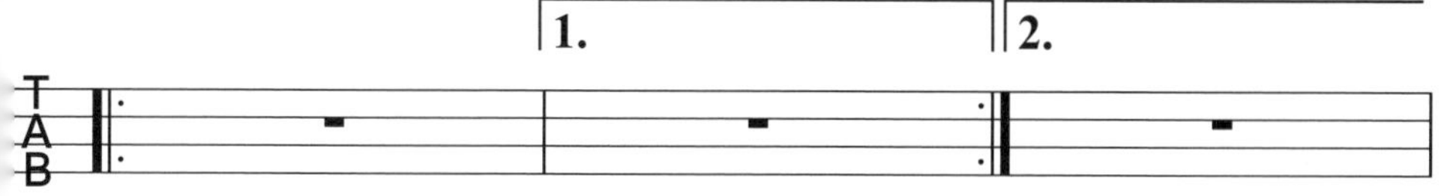

Tuning your ukulele

The ukulele is unusual among string instruments in that the strings are not tuned in order of pitch. Watch out for this!
Here are the tuning notes for a ukulele on a piano keyboard:

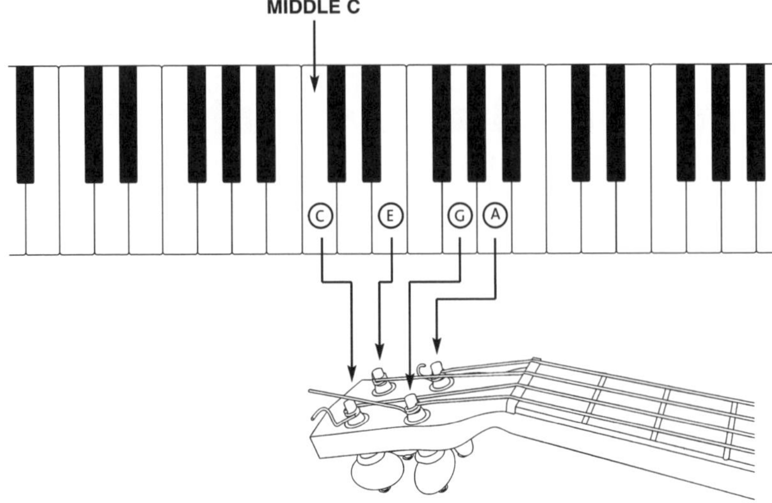

A good way to remember the notes of the ukulele's strings is this little tune:

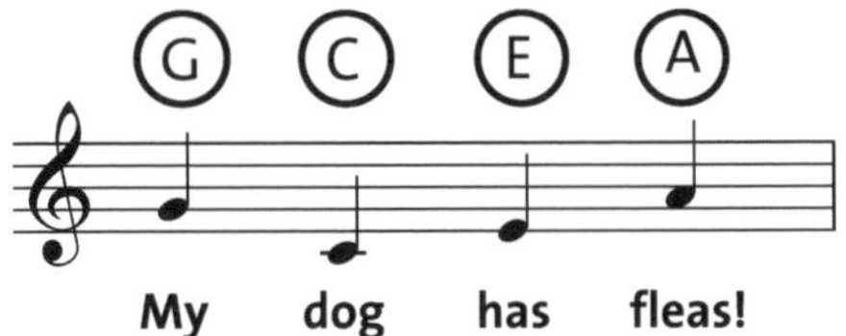

Reading chord boxes

Chord boxes are diagrams of the ukulele neck viewed head upwards, face on as illustrated. The top horizontal line is the nut, unless a higher fret number is indicated, the others are the frets.

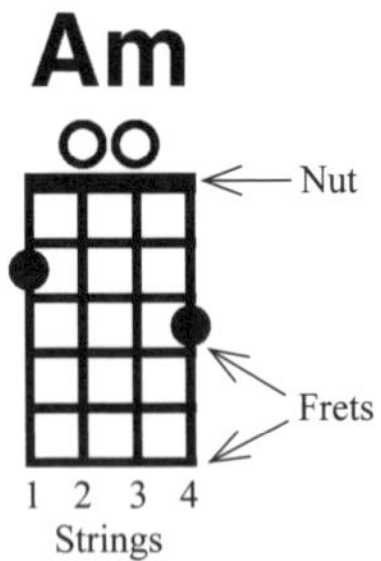

The vertical lines are the strings, starting from G (or 4th) on the left to A (or 1st) on the right.

The black dots indicate where to place your fingers.

Strings marked with an O are played open, not fretted. Strings marked with an X should not be played.

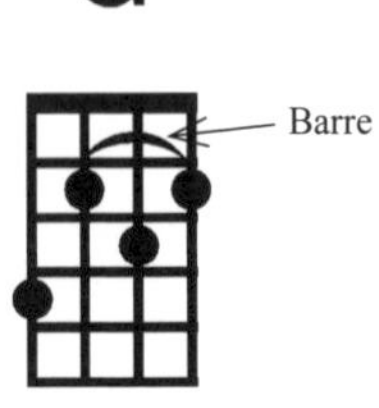

The curved bracket indicates a 'barre' – hold down the strings under the bracket with your first finger, using your fingers to fret the remaining notes.

N.C. = No chord.

Abraham, Martin & John

Words & Music by Dick Holler

Intro | B♭ | Dm | E♭ | B♭ ||
Mm.

Verse 1

B♭ Dm
Has anybody here,
E♭ B♭
Seen my old friend Abraham,
Cm7 F7sus4 F7
Can you tell me, where he's gone?
Gm Dm
Oh,__ he freed a lot of people,
E♭ B♭
But it seems the good die young, yeah.
Cm7 F7sus4 B♭
I just looked a - round and he was gone, ooh.

Verse 2

B♭ Dm
Has anybody here,
E♭ B♭
Seen my old friend John,
Cm7 F7sus4 F7
Can you tell me where he's gone?__
Gm Dm
You know, he freed a lot of people,
E♭ B♭
But it seems the good die young, yeah.
Cm7 F7sus4 B♭
I just looked a - round and he was gone, oh yeah.

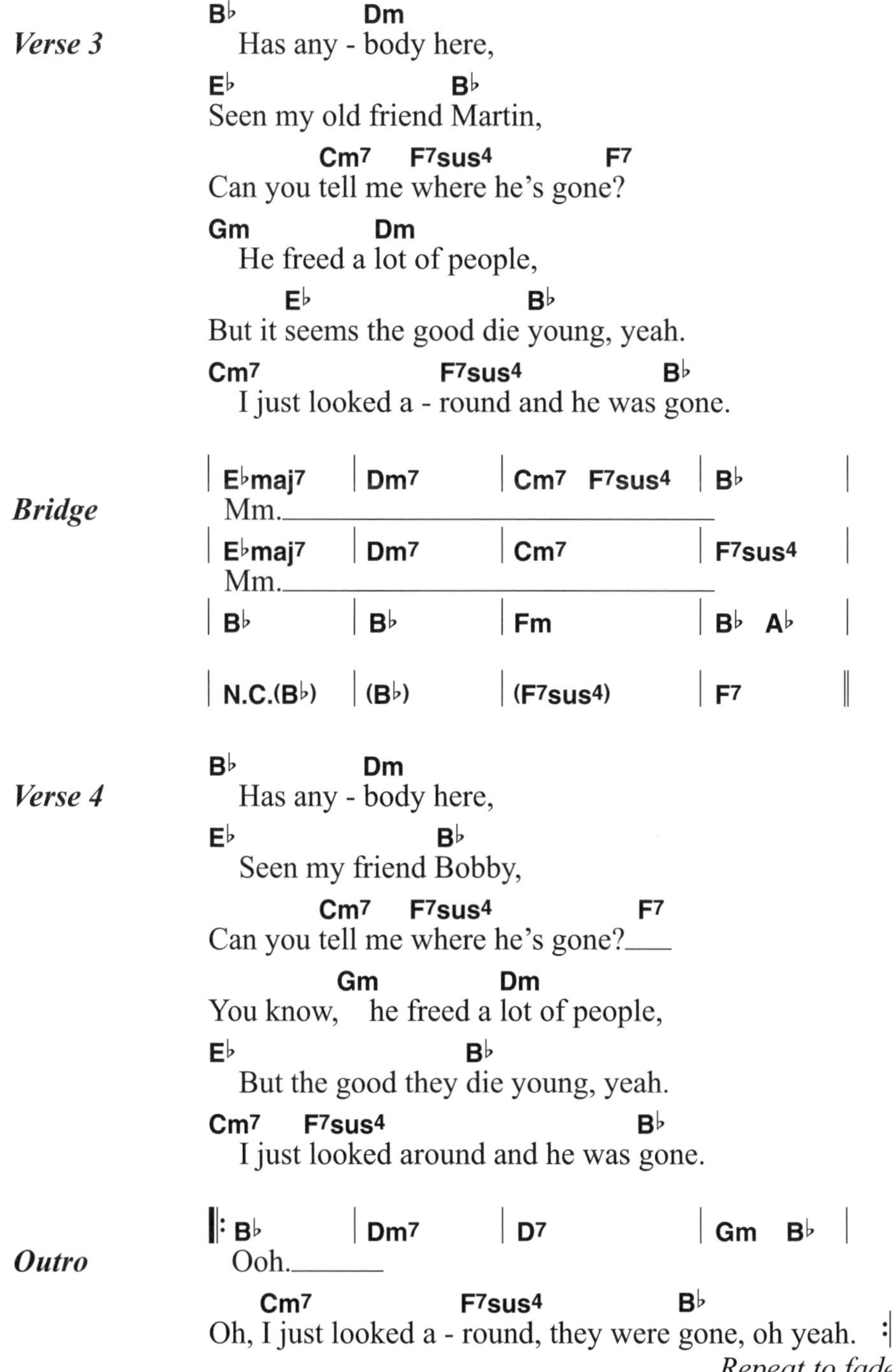

Verse 3
B♭ Dm
Has any - body here,
E♭ B♭
Seen my old friend Martin,
Cm7 F7sus4 F7
Can you tell me where he's gone?
Gm Dm
He freed a lot of people,
E♭ B♭
But it seems the good die young, yeah.
Cm7 F7sus4 B♭
I just looked a - round and he was gone.
Bridge
| E♭maj7 | Dm7 | Cm7 F7sus4 | B♭ |
Mm.
| E♭maj7 | Dm7 | Cm7 | F7sus4 |
Mm.
| B♭ | B♭ | Fm | B♭ A♭ |
| N.C.(B♭) | (B♭) | (F7sus4) | F7 ||
Verse 4
B♭ Dm
Has any - body here,
E♭ B♭
Seen my friend Bobby,
Cm7 F7sus4 F7
Can you tell me where he's gone?
Gm Dm
You know, he freed a lot of people,
E♭ B♭
But the good they die young, yeah.
Cm7 F7sus4 B♭
I just looked around and he was gone.
Outro
|: B♭ | Dm7 | D7 | Gm B♭ |
Ooh.
Cm7 F7sus4 B♭
Oh, I just looked a - round, they were gone, oh yeah. :|
Repeat to fade

Across 110th Street

Words & Music by Bobby Womack & J.J. Johnson

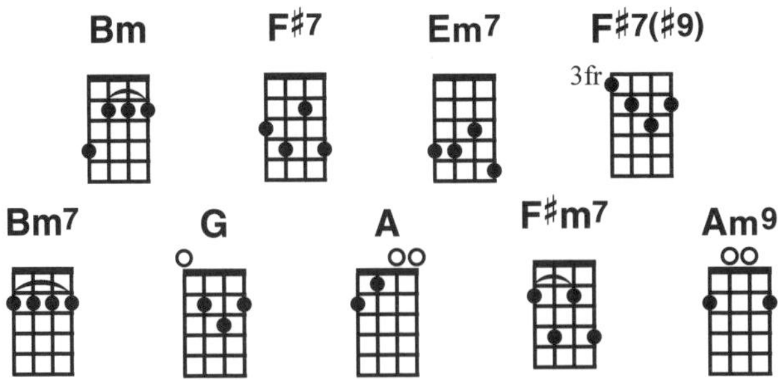

To match original recording, tune ukulele slightly flat

Intro

| Bm | Bm | F♯7 | F♯7 |

| Bm | Bm | F♯7 | F♯7 |

| Bm | Bm | Em7 | F♯7(♯9) |
Ooh.________________________

| Bm | Bm | Em7 | F♯7(♯9) ||
Ooh.________________________

Verse 1

Em7
I was the third brother of five,
Bm7
Do - ing whatever I had to do to survive.
Em7
I'm not saying what I did was alright,
Bm7
Trying to break out of the ghetto was a day to day fight.
Em7
Been down so long, getting up didn't cross my mind,
Bm7
I knew there was a better way of life that I was just trying to find.
Em7
You don't know what you'll do until you're put under pressure,
Bm7
Across a Hundred-and-tenth Street is a hell of a tester.

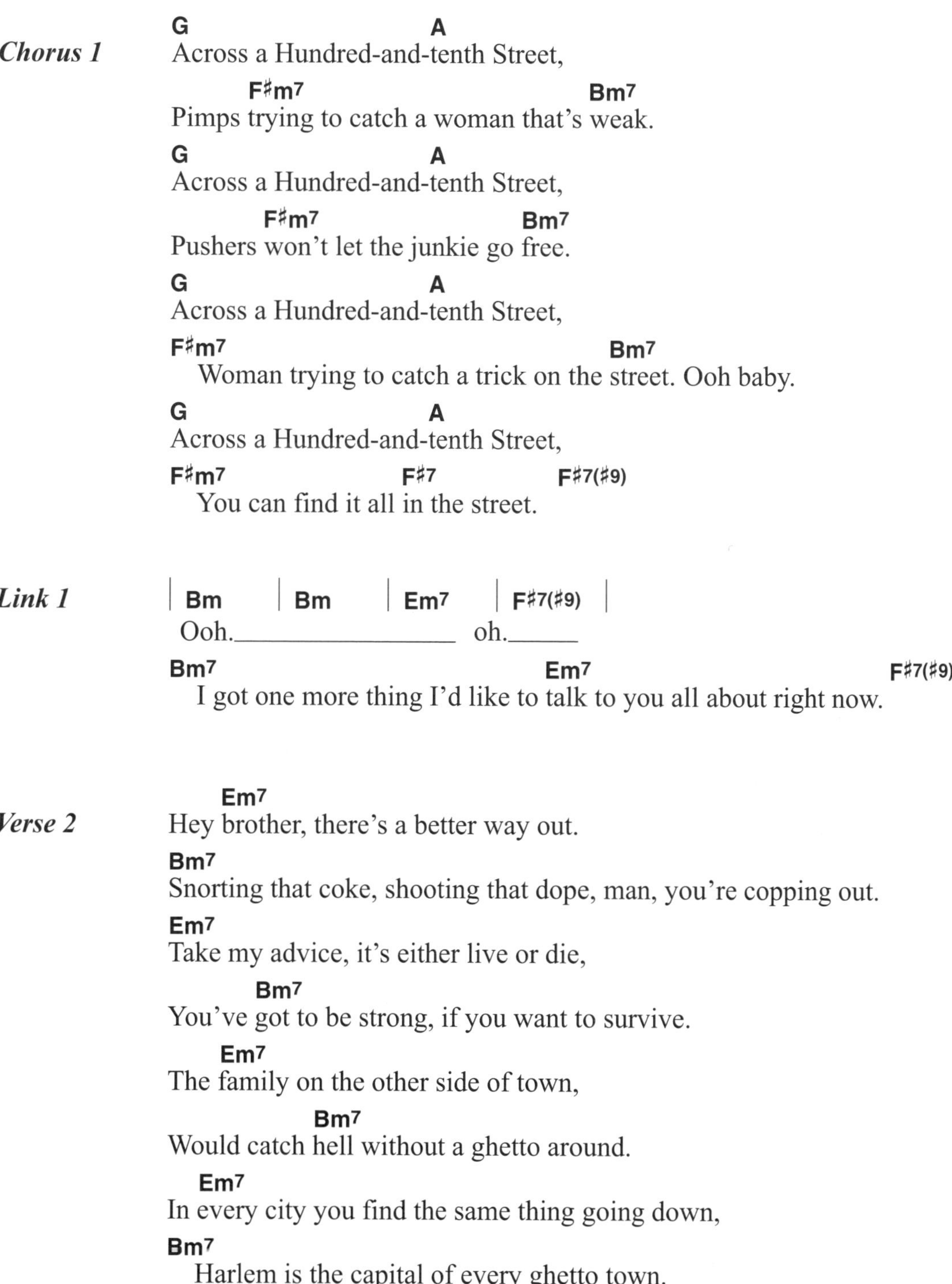

Chorus 1

G A
Across a Hundred-and-tenth Street,
F♯m7 Bm7
Pimps trying to catch a woman that's weak.
G A
Across a Hundred-and-tenth Street,
F♯m7 Bm7
Pushers won't let the junkie go free.
G A
Across a Hundred-and-tenth Street,
F♯m7 Bm7
Woman trying to catch a trick on the street. Ooh baby.
G A
Across a Hundred-and-tenth Street,
F♯m7 F♯7 F♯7(♯9)
You can find it all in the street.

Link 1

| Bm | Bm | Em7 | F♯7(♯9) |
Ooh.________________ oh.______
Bm7 Em7 F♯7(♯9)
I got one more thing I'd like to talk to you all about right now.

Verse 2

Em7
Hey brother, there's a better way out.
Bm7
Snorting that coke, shooting that dope, man, you're copping out.
Em7
Take my advice, it's either live or die,
Bm7
You've got to be strong, if you want to survive.
Em7
The family on the other side of town,
Bm7
Would catch hell without a ghetto around.
Em7
In every city you find the same thing going down,
Bm7
Harlem is the capital of every ghetto town.

Chorus 2

```
G                          A
Across a Hundred-and-tenth Street,
          F♯m7                                   Bm7
Pimps trying to catch a woman that's weak.
G                          A
Across a Hundred-and-tenth Street,
            F♯m7                         Bm7
Pushers won't let the junkie go free.
G                          A
Across a Hundred-and-tenth Street,
            F♯m7                                 Bm7
Woman trying to catch a trick on the street. Ooh baby.
G                          A
Across a Hundred-and-tenth Street,
             F♯m7       F♯7  F♯7(♯9)       Bm
You can find it all__________ in the street, yes you can.
Em7                 F♯7(♯9)
   Oh, look a - round you, look around you,
                                  Em7                   Em7   F♯7(♯9)
Look around you, look a - round you, ah, yeah.
Am(add9)
   Ooh.
```

The Fez

Words & Music by Donald Fagen, Walter Becker & Paul Griffin

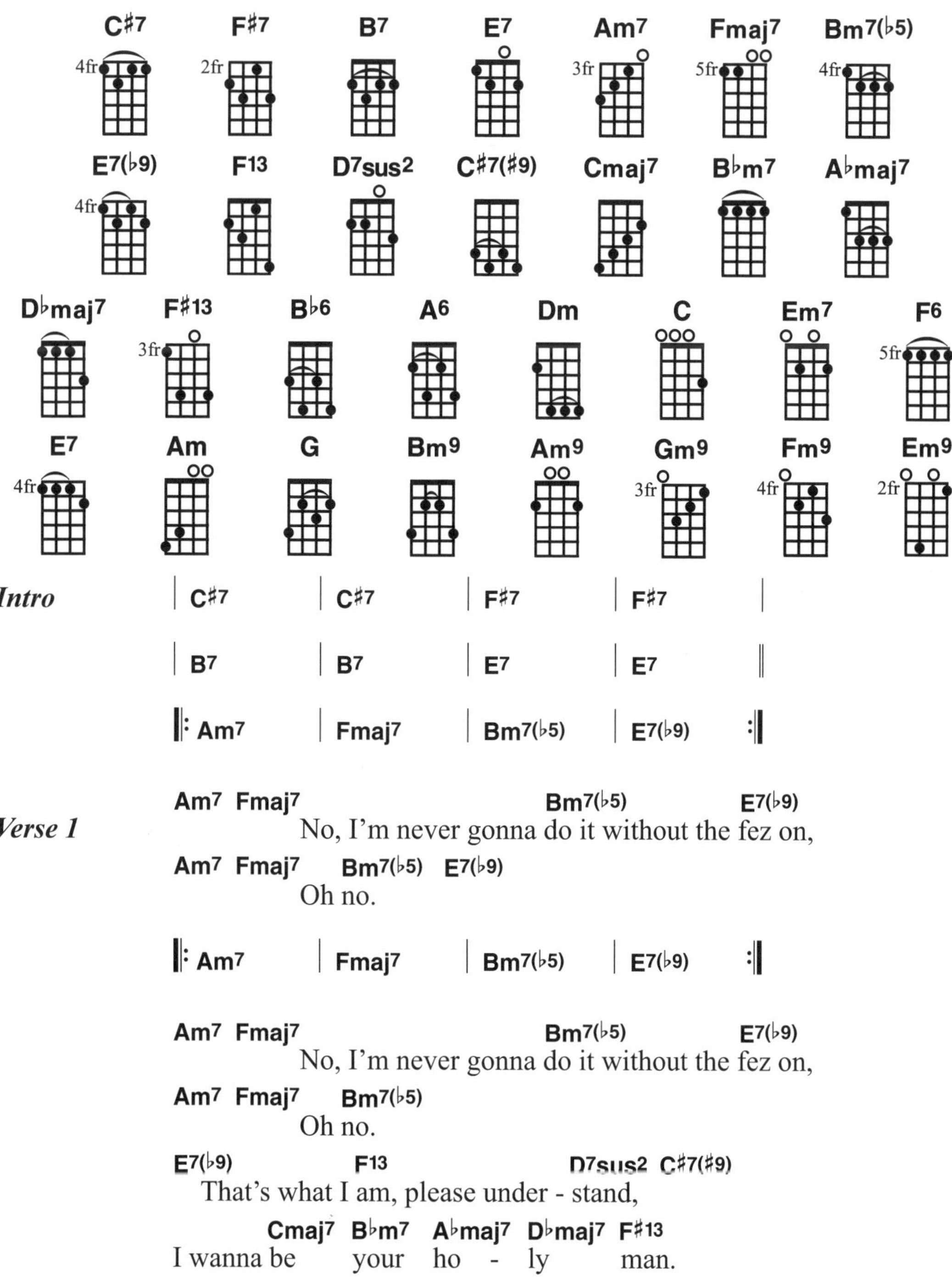

Link 1 | B7 | B7 | E7 | E7 ||

Instrumental 1 |: Am7 | Fmaj7 | Bm7(♭5) | E7(♭9) :|

Verse 2

Am7 Fmaj7 Bm7(♭5) E7(♭9)
No, I'm never gonna do it without the fez on,
Am7 Fmaj7 Bm7(♭5) E7(♭9)
Oh no.

|: Am7 | Fmaj7 | Bm7(♭5) | E7(♭9) :|

Am7 Fmaj7 Bm7(♭5) E7(♭9)
Ain't never gonna do it without the fez on,
Am7 Fmaj7 Bm7(♭5)
Oh no.
E7(♭9) F13 D7sus2 C♯7(♯9)
That's what I am, please under - stand,
Cmaj7 B♭m7 A♭maj7 D♭maj7 F♯13
I wanna be your ho - ly man.

Instrumental 2

B♭6 A6	B♭6	Dm C	B7
Cmaj7	Cmaj7	Em7	Em7
Cmaj7	Cmaj7	Em7	Em7
F6 E7*	F6	Am G	F♯7
Bm9 Am9	Gm9 Fm9	Em9	Am7
B7	B7	E7	E7	
: Am7	Fmaj7	Bm7(♭5)	E7(♭9) :

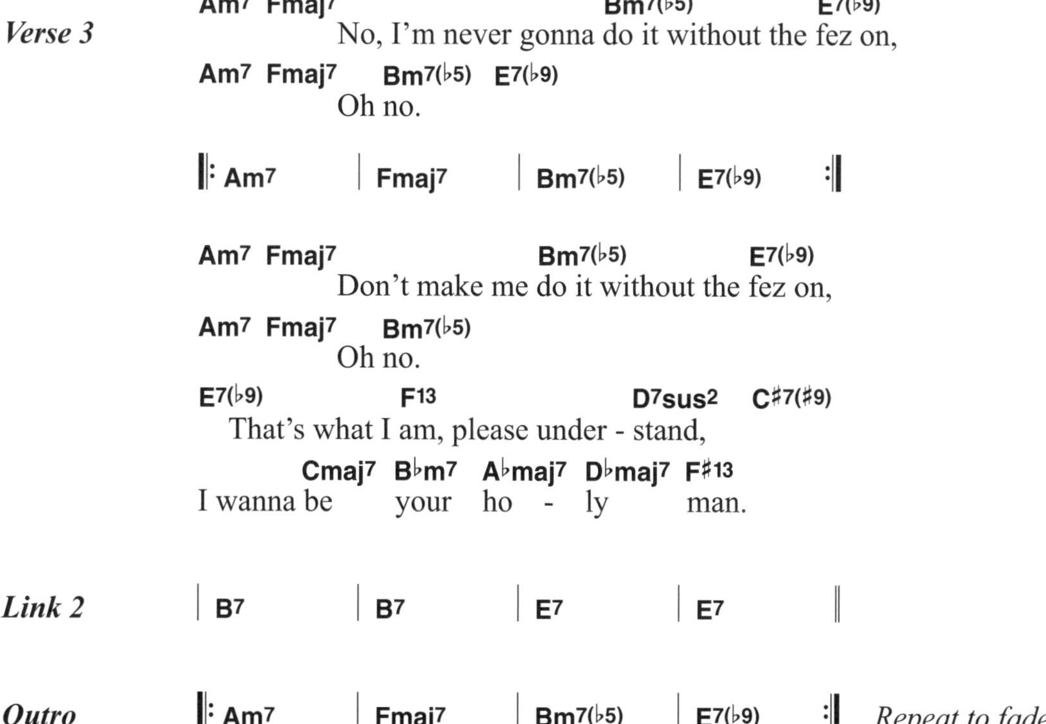

Verse 3

Am7 Fmaj7 Bm7(♭5) E7(♭9)
No, I'm never gonna do it without the fez on,
Am7 Fmaj7 Bm7(♭5) E7(♭9)
Oh no.

|: Am7 | Fmaj7 | Bm7(♭5) | E7(♭9) :|

Am7 Fmaj7 Bm7(♭5) E7(♭9)
Don't make me do it without the fez on,
Am7 Fmaj7 Bm7(♭5)
Oh no.
E7(♭9) F13 D7sus2 C♯7(♯9)
That's what I am, please under - stand,
Cmaj7 B♭m7 A♭maj7 D♭maj7 F♯13
I wanna be your ho - ly man.

Link 2 | B7 | B7 | E7 | E7 ||

Outro |: Am7 | Fmaj7 | Bm7(♭5) | E7(♭9) :| *Repeat to fade*

Aht Uh Mi Hed

Words & Music by Shuggie Otis

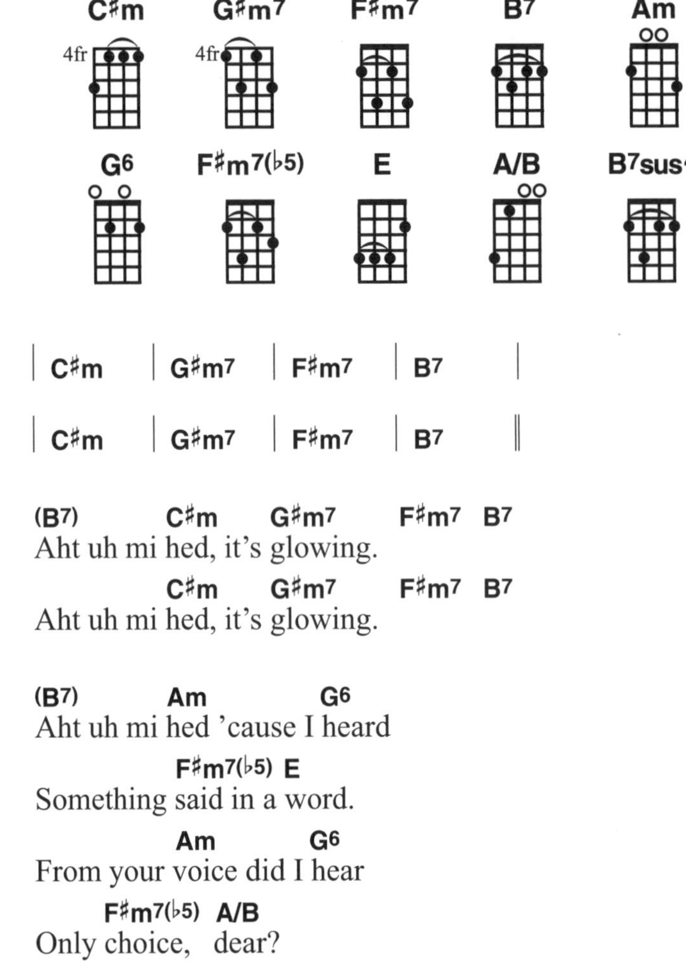

Intro | C♯m | G♯m7 | F♯m7 | B7 |

| C♯m | G♯m7 | F♯m7 | B7 ||

Chorus 1

(B7) C♯m G♯m7 F♯m7 B7
Aht uh mi hed, it's glowing.
C♯m G♯m7 F♯m7 B7
Aht uh mi hed, it's glowing.

Verse 1

(B7) Am G6
Aht uh mi hed 'cause I heard
F♯m7(♭5) E
Something said in a word.
Am G6
From your voice did I hear
F♯m7(♭5) A/B
Only choice, dear?

Chorus 2

(B7) C♯m G♯m7
Aht uh mi hed, je t'aime,
F♯m7 B7 C♯m G♯m7 F♯m7 B7
From shots that shot above.___
C♯m G♯m7 F♯m7 B7
Aht uh mi hed things are different

Verse 2

(B7)   Am   G6
Aht uh mi hed all the time,

F♯m7(♭5)   E
In the bed for a rhyme.

Am   G6
Flashing back to your air

F♯m7(♭5)   A/B
And the good   there.

Instrumental 𝄆 C♯m | G♯m7 | F♯m7 | B7 𝄇 *Play 3 times*

Verse 3

Am   G6
There magic too,

F♯m7(♭5)   E
When the spread is on you.

Am   G6
Won't you read me a trip

F♯m7(♭5)   A/B   C♯m7
From your whip   here, who?______

Outro

G♯m7
It's about time for something new,

F♯m7   B7sus4
You got to grow, got to grow.

C♯m7   G♯m7   F♯m7   B7sus4
Aht uh mi hed.

C♯m7   G♯m7   F♯m7   B7sus4
Aht uh mi hed.

C♯m7   G♯m7   F♯m7   B7sus4
Said, hed, ah hed,   hed, glowing.

C♯m7   G♯m7   F♯m7   B7sus4
Oh, I wanna tell you.

C♯m7
Hed, aht uh mi hed,

G♯m7
Aht uh mi hed, aht uh mi hed,

F♯m7   B7sus4
Aht uh mi hed, you got the glowing.

𝄆 C♯m | G♯m7 | F♯m7 | B7sus4 𝄇 *Play 5 times*

California Soul

Words & Music by Nickolas Ashford & Valerie Simpson

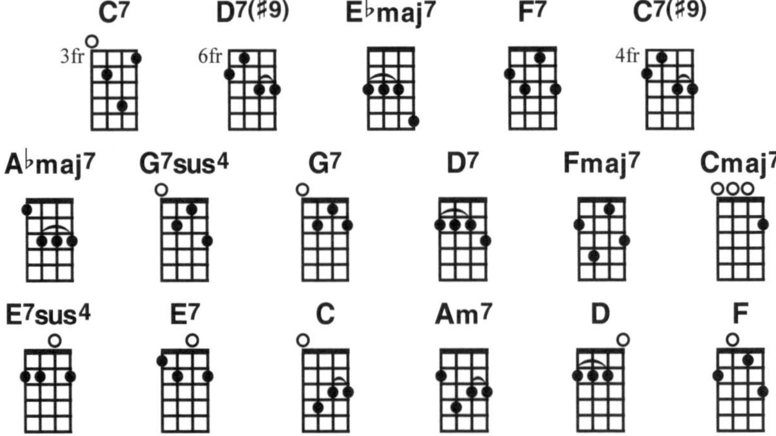

To match original recording, tune ukulele up one semitone

Intro | C7 | D7(#9) | E♭maj7 | F7 |
| C7 | N.C. | N.C. | N.C. ||

Verse 1

```
N.C.   C7                          D7(#9)
Like a sound you hear that lingers in your ear,
E♭maj7                        F7          C7       D7(#9)  E♭maj7  F7
But you can't forget from sundown to sunset.
       C7                       D7(#9)
It's all in the air, you hear it everywhere,
E♭maj7                          F7         C7          D7(#9)
No matter what you do it's gonna grab a hold on        you.
E♭maj7  F7       C7(#9)   A♭maj7              G7sus4    G7
   Cali - fornia soul,______ California soul.
```

Bridge 1

```
(G7)          D7                    Fmaj7
They say the sun comes up every morning,
                     D7                  Fmaj7
And if you listen, oh so carefully,
     Cmaj7      C7         Fmaj7
The winds that ride on the high tide
D7                 E7sus4
Whistles a melo - dy.
```

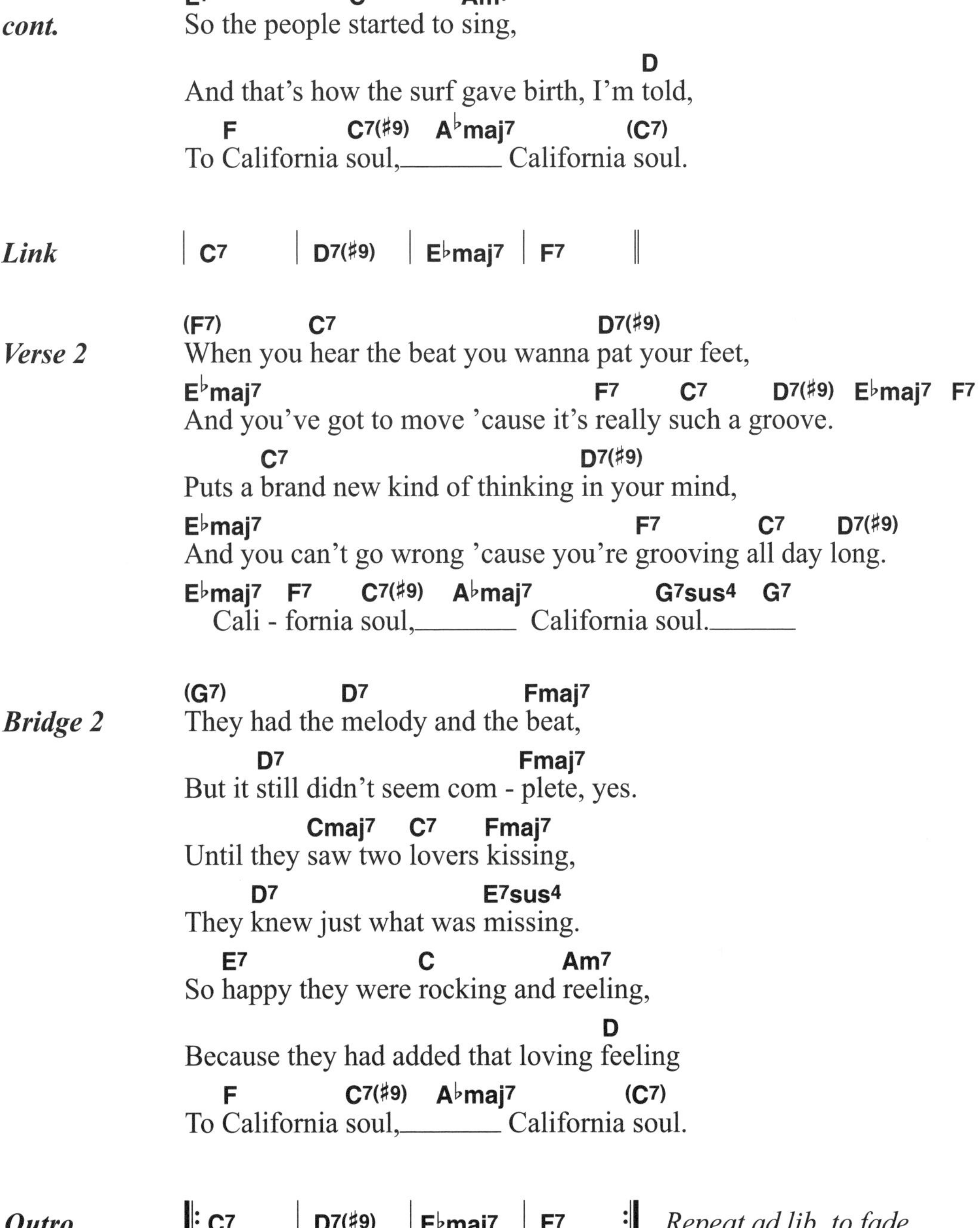

cont.

E7 C Am7
So the people started to sing,
D
And that's how the surf gave birth, I'm told,
F C7(♯9) A♭maj7 (C7)
To California soul,_______ California soul.

Link

| C7 | D7(♯9) | E♭maj7 | F7 ||

Verse 2

(F7) C7 D7(♯9)
When you hear the beat you wanna pat your feet,
E♭maj7 F7 C7 D7(♯9) E♭maj7 F7
And you've got to move 'cause it's really such a groove.
C7 D7(♯9)
Puts a brand new kind of thinking in your mind,
E♭maj7 F7 C7 D7(♯9)
And you can't go wrong 'cause you're grooving all day long.
E♭maj7 F7 C7(♯9) A♭maj7 G7sus4 G7
Cali - fornia soul,_______ California soul._______

Bridge 2

(G7) D7 Fmaj7
They had the melody and the beat,
D7 Fmaj7
But it still didn't seem com - plete, yes.
Cmaj7 C7 Fmaj7
Until they saw two lovers kissing,
D7 E7sus4
They knew just what was missing.
E7 C Am7
So happy they were rocking and reeling,
D
Because they had added that loving feeling
F C7(♯9) A♭maj7 (C7)
To California soul,_______ California soul.

Outro

|: C7 | D7(♯9) | E♭maj7 | F7 :| *Repeat ad lib. to fade*

Easy

Words & Music by Lionel Richie

Ab Cm7 Bbm7 Eb7sus4 Gb Db
Gbmaj7 Ebm7 Ab7sus4 Bm7 A C#m7 E7sus4

Intro

| Ab | Cm7 | Bbm7 | Eb7sus4 |
| Ab | Cm7 | Bbm7 | Bbm7 ||

Verse 1

```
Ab                  Cm7                   Bbm7          Eb7sus4
  Know it sounds funny, but I just can't stand the pain,
Ab         Cm7                  Bbm7   Eb7sus4
  Girl, I'm leaving you tomor - row.
Ab         Cm7                          Bbm7       Eb7sus4
  Seems to me girl you know I've done all I can,
Ab         Cm7                  Bbm7             Eb7sus4
  You see I begged, stole and I borrowed, yeah.
```

Chorus 1

```
(Eb7sus4)                Ab      Cm7   Bbm7
Ooh, that's why I'm ea - sy,
   Eb7sus4                      Ab     Cm7   Bbm7
I'm easy like Sunday morn - ing.
Eb7sus4                 Ab    Cm7   Bbm7
  That's why I'm ea - sy,________
   Eb7sus4               Gb   Db  Eb7sus4  Ab
I'm easy like Sunday morn         -        ing.
```

Verse 2

```
Ab              Cm7                        Bbm7           Eb7sus4
  Why in the world would anybody put chains on me?
Ab      Cm7                    Bbm7   Eb7sus4
  I've paid my dues to make it.
Ab              Cm7                        Bbm7           Eb7sus4
  Everybody wants me to be what they want me to be,
Ab            Cm7                 Bbm7         Eb7sus4
  I'm not happy when I try to fake it, no.
```

Chorus 2 As Chorus 1

Bridge

```
(A♭)          G♭maj7  D♭   E♭m7    A♭7sus4
I wanna be high,     so   high,
           D♭     G♭maj7                          D♭    E♭m7   A♭7sus4
I wan - na be free to know the things I do are   right.
           D♭     G♭maj7
I wan - na be free,
D♭   E♭m7   A♭7sus4
Just me,          whoa, baby.
```

Link

| E♭m7 | G♭ | E♭m7 | D♭ | D♭ ||

Guitar solo

| A♭ | Cm7 | B♭m7 | E♭7sus4 |

| A♭ | Cm7 | B♭m7 | E♭7sus4 |

| A♭ | Cm7 | B♭m7 | E♭7sus4 |

| A♭ | Cm7 | B♭m7 | B♭m7 ||

Chorus 3

```
(B♭m7)              A♭     Cm7   B♭m7
That's why I'm easy,
    E♭7sus4                       A♭   Cm7    B♭m7
I'm easy like Sunday morn - ing, yeah.
E♭7sus4                    A♭     Cm7  B♭m7
   That's why I'm ea - sy,__________
    E♭7sus4                 A♭       Cm7          B♭m7   Bm7
I'm easy like Sunday morning,____ whoa.____
```

Chorus 4

```
(Bm7)        A  C♯m7    Bm7
'Cause I'm ea    -   sy,
E7sus4                     A      C♯m7       Bm7
Easy like Sunday morning,        yeah.____
E7sus4            A          C♯m7   Bm7
   'Cause I'm easy,
E7sus4                     A        C♯m7       Bm7
Easy like Sunday morning,        whoa.____        To fade
```

(Fallin' Like) Dominoes

Words & Music by Harold Clayton, Mbaji & Sigidi

G♯m7 C♯m7 Amaj7 Emaj7 A/B B7

Intro |: N.C.(G♯m7) | N.C.(C♯m7) | N.C.(G♯m7) | N.C.(C♯m7) :|

|: G♯m7 | C♯m7 | G♯m7 | C♯m7 :|

Verse 1

```
G♯m7                                                          C♯m7
   A-pretty baby, dry your eyes, don't you know it can't be that bad.
G♯m7                                                             C♯m7
   Oh, how it hurts me, pretty baby, when I see you sitting there so sad.
G♯m7                                                   C♯m7
   No need to worry about tomorrow and yester - day is gone.
G♯m7
   So raise your chin up girl,
                                        C♯m7
And we will work our problems out one by one.
```

Chorus 1

```
Amaj7                                       Emaj7
Hold me tight, (hold me tight), don't let go,
Amaj7                          Emaj7
Turn me loose, never no, no, no.
       Amaj7                          Emaj7
We'll stand our problems all in a row,
Amaj7                          Emaj7
Watch them fall like domi - noes,
             (Amaj7)
Falling like dominoes.
```

Instrumental 1 |: Amaj7 | Emaj7 | Amaj7 | Emaj7 :|

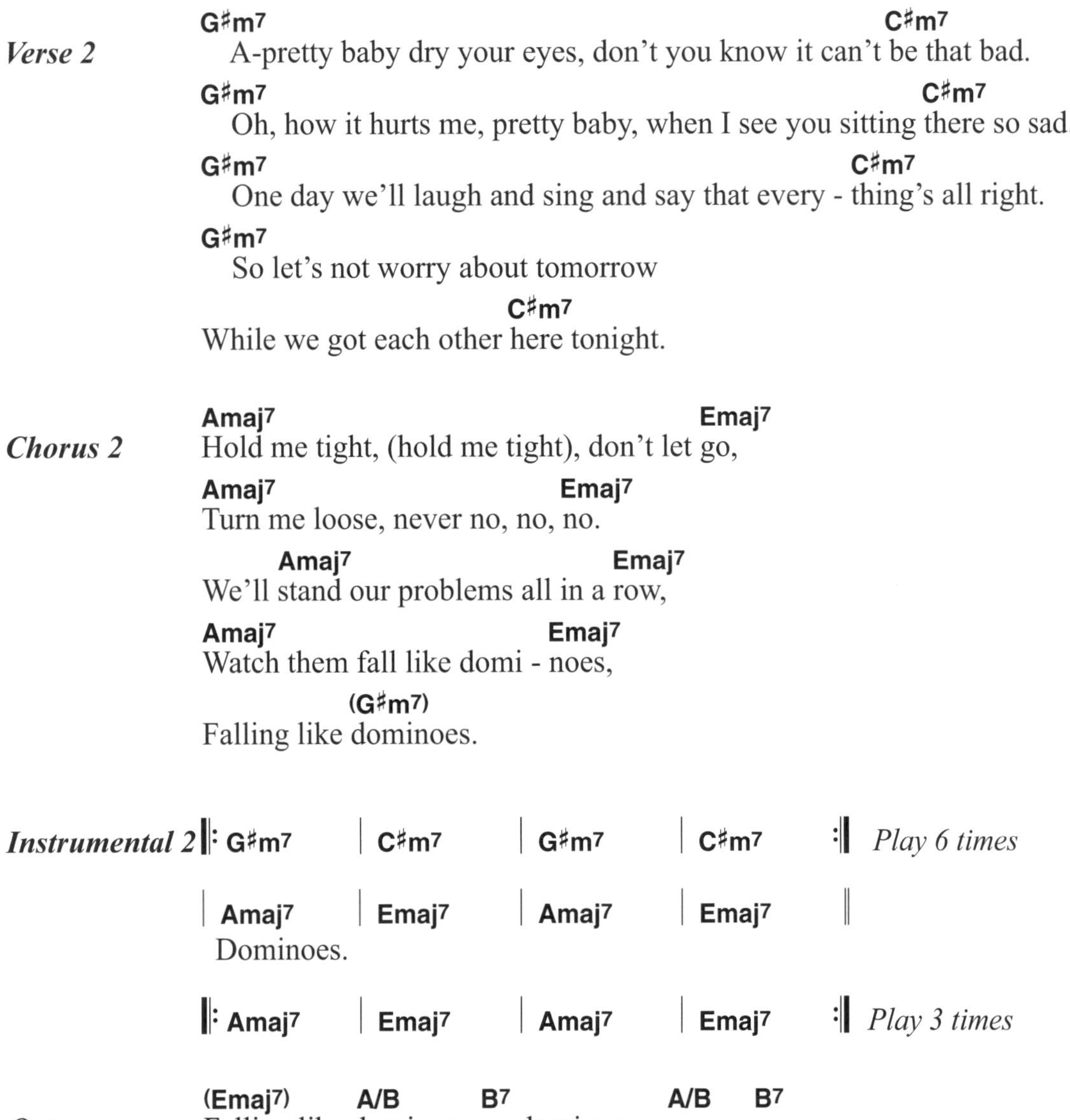

Verse 2

G♯m7 C♯m7
A-pretty baby dry your eyes, don't you know it can't be that bad.

G♯m7 C♯m7
Oh, how it hurts me, pretty baby, when I see you sitting there so sad.

G♯m7 C♯m7
One day we'll laugh and sing and say that every - thing's all right.

G♯m7
So let's not worry about tomorrow

C♯m7
While we got each other here tonight.

Chorus 2

Amaj7 Emaj7
Hold me tight, (hold me tight), don't let go,

Amaj7 Emaj7
Turn me loose, never no, no, no.

Amaj7 Emaj7
We'll stand our problems all in a row,

Amaj7 Emaj7
Watch them fall like domi - noes,

(G♯m7)
Falling like dominoes.

Instrumental 2

𝄆 G♯m7 | C♯m7 | G♯m7 | C♯m7 𝄇 *Play 6 times*

| Amaj7 | Emaj7 | Amaj7 | Emaj7 ‖
Dominoes.

𝄆 Amaj7 | Emaj7 | Amaj7 | Emaj7 𝄇 *Play 3 times*

Outro

(Emaj7) A/B B7 A/B B7
Falling like dominoes, dominoes.

𝄆 A/B | B7 | A/B | B7 |

(B7) A/B B7 A/B B7
Falling like dominoes, dominoes. 𝄇 *Repeat to fade*

Family Affair

Words & Music by Sylvester Stewart

Dm7 Bbmaj7 F Gm7 C7 D7(#9) D7 A7

Intro | Dm7 | Dm7 ||

```
Dm7                        Bbmaj7  F              Gm7    C7
It's a family affair,      it's a family af - fair.
Dm7                           Bbmaj7  F              Gm7    C7
   It's a family affair,      it's a family af - fair.
```

Verse 1

```
Gm7        C7                        Gm7
   One child grows up to be
                   C7
Somebody that just loves to learn
             Gm7     C7                        Gm7
And an - other child grows up to be
                           C7
Somebody you'd just love to burn.
Gm7        C7                Gm7
   Mom loves the both of them,
                        C7
You see it's in the blood.
Gm7              C7
   Both kids    are good to Mom,
Gm7                     C7
Blood's thicker than mud.
                     Gm7                       C7
It's a family af - fair, (it's a family af - fair.)
                     Gm7
It's a family af - fair, (it's a family affair.)
D7(#9)    D7
No, no, they're one of them.
```

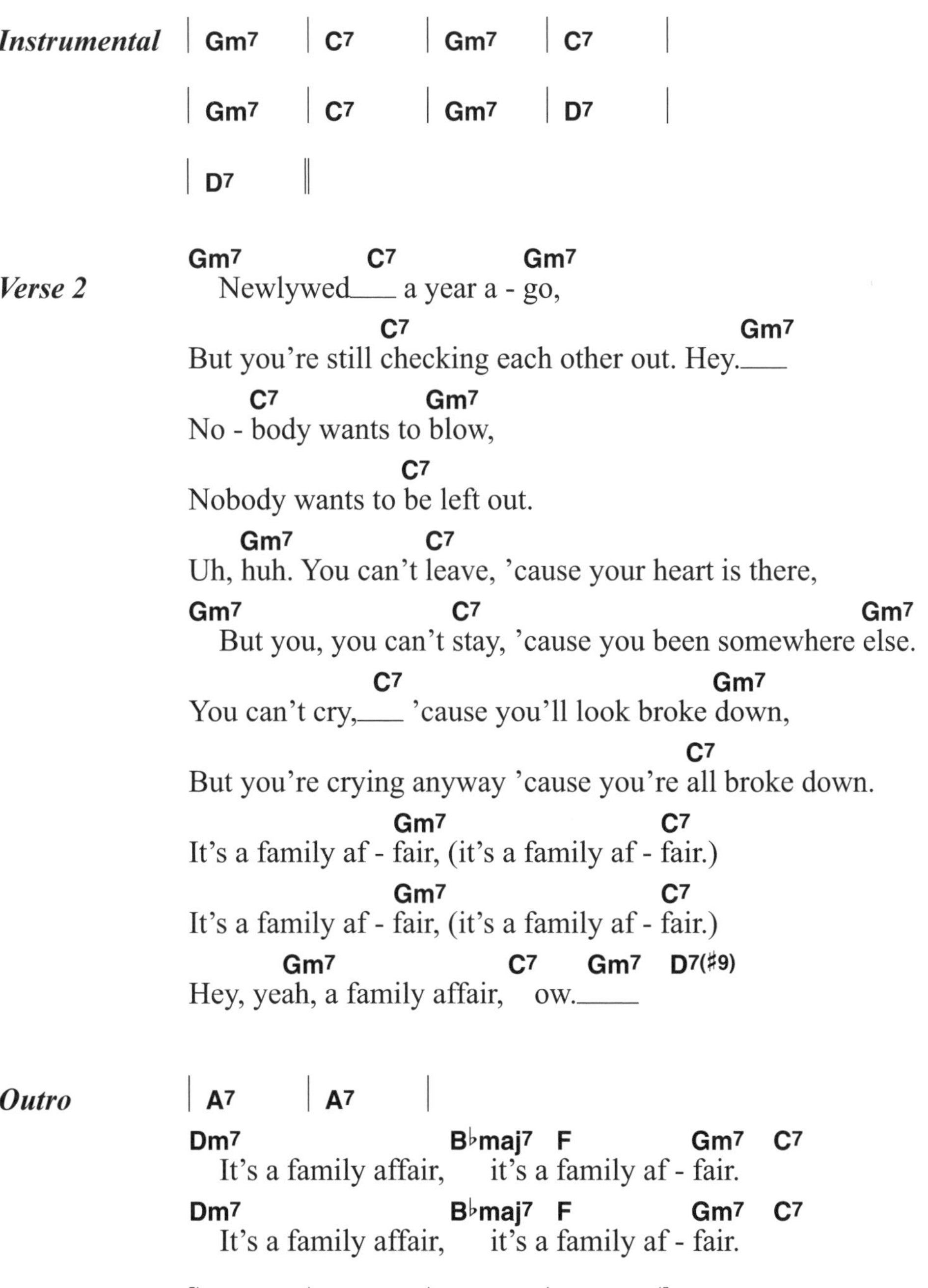

Instrumental
Gm7	C7	Gm7	C7
Gm7	C7	Gm7	D7
D7	
Verse 2
Gm7 C7 Gm7
Newlywed___ a year a - go,
C7 Gm7
But you're still checking each other out. Hey.___
C7 Gm7
No - body wants to blow,
C7
Nobody wants to be left out.
Gm7 C7
Uh, huh. You can't leave, 'cause your heart is there,
Gm7 C7 Gm7
But you, you can't stay, 'cause you been somewhere else.
C7 Gm7
You can't cry,___ 'cause you'll look broke down,
C7
But you're crying anyway 'cause you're all broke down.
Gm7 C7
It's a family af - fair, (it's a family af - fair.)
Gm7 C7
It's a family af - fair, (it's a family af - fair.)
Gm7 C7 Gm7 D7(♯9)
Hey, yeah, a family affair, ow.___
Outro
A7	A7
Dm7 B♭maj7 F Gm7 C7
It's a family affair, it's a family af - fair.
Dm7 B♭maj7 F Gm7 C7
It's a family affair, it's a family af - fair.
|: Gm7	C7	Gm7	C7 :|| Repeat to fade

I Get The Sweetest Feeling

Words & Music by Van McCoy & Alicia Evelyn

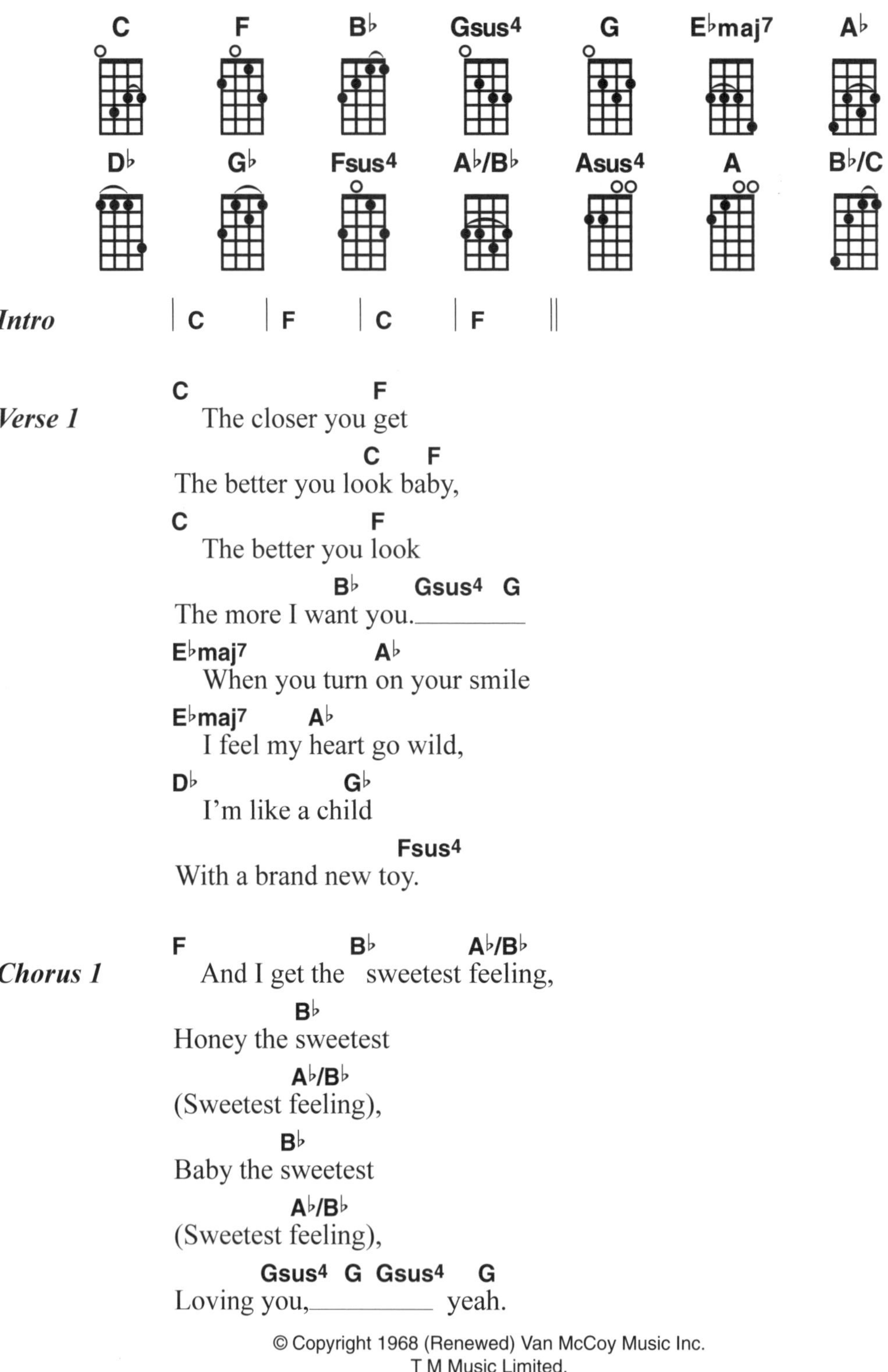

Intro | C | F | C | F ||

Verse 1

C   F
   The closer you get
                                C   F
The better you look baby,
C   F
   The better you look
                          B♭   Gsus4   G
The more I want you.________
E♭maj7   A♭
   When you turn on your smile
E♭maj7   A♭
   I feel my heart go wild,
D♭   G♭
   I'm like a child
                                   Fsus4
With a brand new toy.

Chorus 1

F   B♭   A♭/B♭
   And I get the sweetest feeling,
                       B♭
Honey the sweetest
                        A♭/B♭
(Sweetest feeling),
                    B♭
Baby the sweetest
                     A♭/B♭
(Sweetest feeling),
                  Gsus4 G Gsus4   G
Loving you,________ yeah.

Verse 2

```
C                          F
     The warmer your kiss
                             C       F
The deeper you touch me baby,
C                        F
     The deeper your touch
                 B♭              Gsus4  G
The more you thrill me.________
E♭maj7              A♭
     It's more than I can stand
E♭maj7                 A♭
     Girl, when you hold my hand,
D♭                  G♭
     I feel so grand
                   Fsus4
That I could cry.____
```

Chorus 2

```
F
     And I get the
B♭                 A♭/B♭
     (Sweetest feeling),
                B♭
Mamma the sweetest
              A♭/B♭
(Sweetest feeling),
             B♭
Baby the sweetest
               A♭/B♭
 (Sweetest feeling),
          Gsus4  G  Gsus4    G
Loving you._____________
```

Instrumental

```
| C        | B♭       | C        | B♭       |
| C        | B♭       | Asus4  A | Gsus4  G ||
```

Verse 3

    C   F
Ooh, the greater your love
                    C   F
The stronger you hold me baby,
C   F
   The stronger your hold
               B♭   Gsus4   G
The more I need you.________
E♭maj7   A♭
   With every passing day
E♭maj7   A♭
   I love you more in every way,
D♭   G♭
   I'm in love to stay
                Fsus4
And I wanna say:

Chorus 3

F
   I get the
B♭   A♭/B♭
   (Sweetest feeling),
            B♭
Baby the sweetest
            A♭/B♭
(Sweetest feeling),
            B♭
Honey the sweetest
            A♭/B♭
(Sweetest feeling),
         Gsus4 G Gsus4   G
Loving you.____________

Outro

C   B♭/C
Ah, (sweetest feeling),
            C
Baby the sweetest
            B♭/C
(Sweetest feeling),
            C
Sweetest, sweetest
            B♭/C
(Sweetest feeling). *To fade*

I Thought It Was You

Words by Melvin Ragin
Music by Herbie Hancock, Jeffrey Cohen & Melvin Ragin

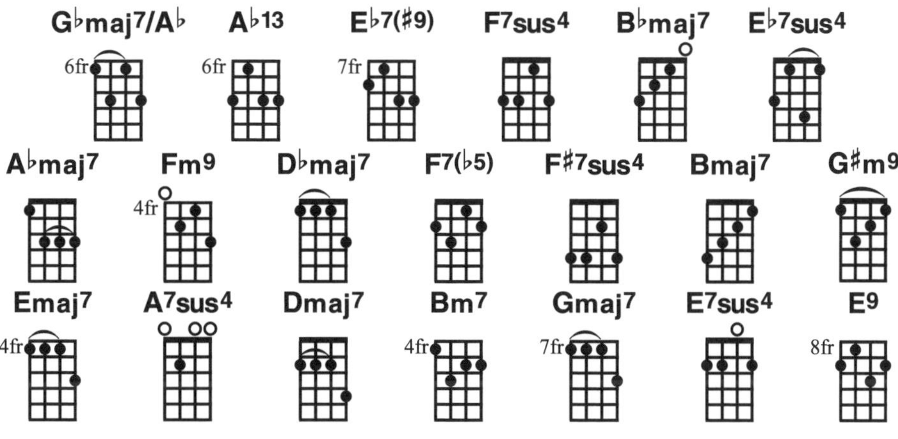

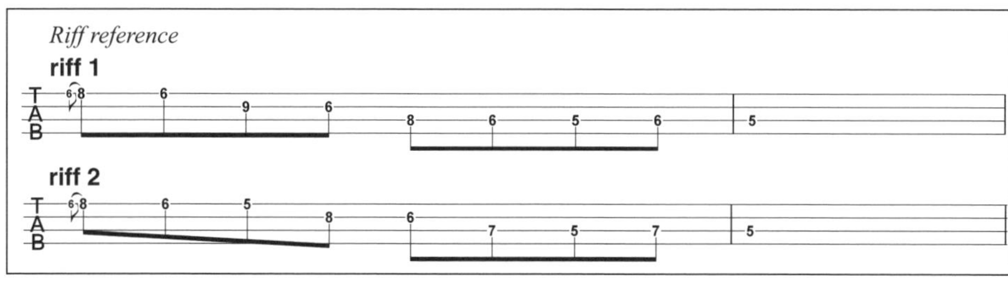

Intro

| N.C. (riff 1) |

|: G♭maj7/A♭ | G♭maj7/A♭ | (w/riff 1)(°2, °4) G♭maj7/A♭ | G♭maj7/A♭ :| *Play 4 times*

| A♭13 | E♭7(♯9/♯5) A♭13 | A♭13 | A♭13 ||

|: A♭13 | E♭7(♯9/♯5) A♭13 | A♭13 | A♭13 :|

| A♭13 | E♭7(♯9/♯5) A♭13 | (w/riff 2) F7sus4 ||

Verse 1

(F7sus4) B♭maj7 E♭7sus4
Just a glance from be - hind,

A♭maj7 Fm9
Happened by chance or de - sign.

D♭maj7 F7(♭5) F♯7sus4
The per - fume she wore

Bmaj7 G♯m9
Took me back through a door

Emaj7 A7sus4
I had closed long ago.

Chorus 1

```
A7sus4
Suddenly,
                    Dmaj7                  Bm7
I thought it was you, thought it was you,
                   Gmaj7                 E7sus4
Thought it was you, thought it was you,
     A7sus4              Dmaj7
Re - member what we knew.

                    Bm7                  Gmaj7
I thought it was you, thought it was you,
                   E7sus4
Thought it was you,
     A7sus4                          Dmaj7   N.C. (w/riff 1)
Re - member when I thought it was you.
```

Instrumental

𝄆 A♭13 | E♭7(♯9/♯5) A♭13 | A♭13 | A♭13 𝄇

Play 20 times ad lib.

Verse 2

```
F7sus4  B♭maj7                          E♭7sus4
We__________ were young, love was new,
        A♭maj7          Fm9
Warm as the sun shin - ing through.
         D♭maj7  F7(♭5)  F♯7sus4
In your arms     it      seemed
        Bmaj7    G♯m9
I went back to a dream
       Emaj7    A7sus4
I had seen long_______ ago.
```

Chorus 2

```
A7sus4
Suddenly,
                    Dmaj7                    Bm7
I thought it was you, I thought it was you,
                    Gmaj7                 E7sus4
I thought it was you, thought it was you,
A7sus4               Dmaj7
I thought we were true.
                    Bm7                   Gmaj7
I thought it was you, thought it was you,
                   Em7
Thought it was you,
      A7sus4                             Dmaj7
Re - member when I thought it was you.
```

Link

| N.C. | N.C. | N.C. | N.C. |

| E9 | E9 | G♭maj7/A♭ | G♭maj7/A♭ | N.C. (w/riff 1)

Outro

```
   A♭13           E♭7(♯9 ♯5)  A♭13
||: Ba-ba-ba-ba-bwee - da, do-da-da-da-da, do-da-da.
A♭13            E♭7(♯9 ♯5)  A♭13
Ba-ba-ba-ba-bwee - da, do-da. :||  Repeat ad lib. to fade
```

I Had A Talk With My Man

Words & Music by James Cleveland

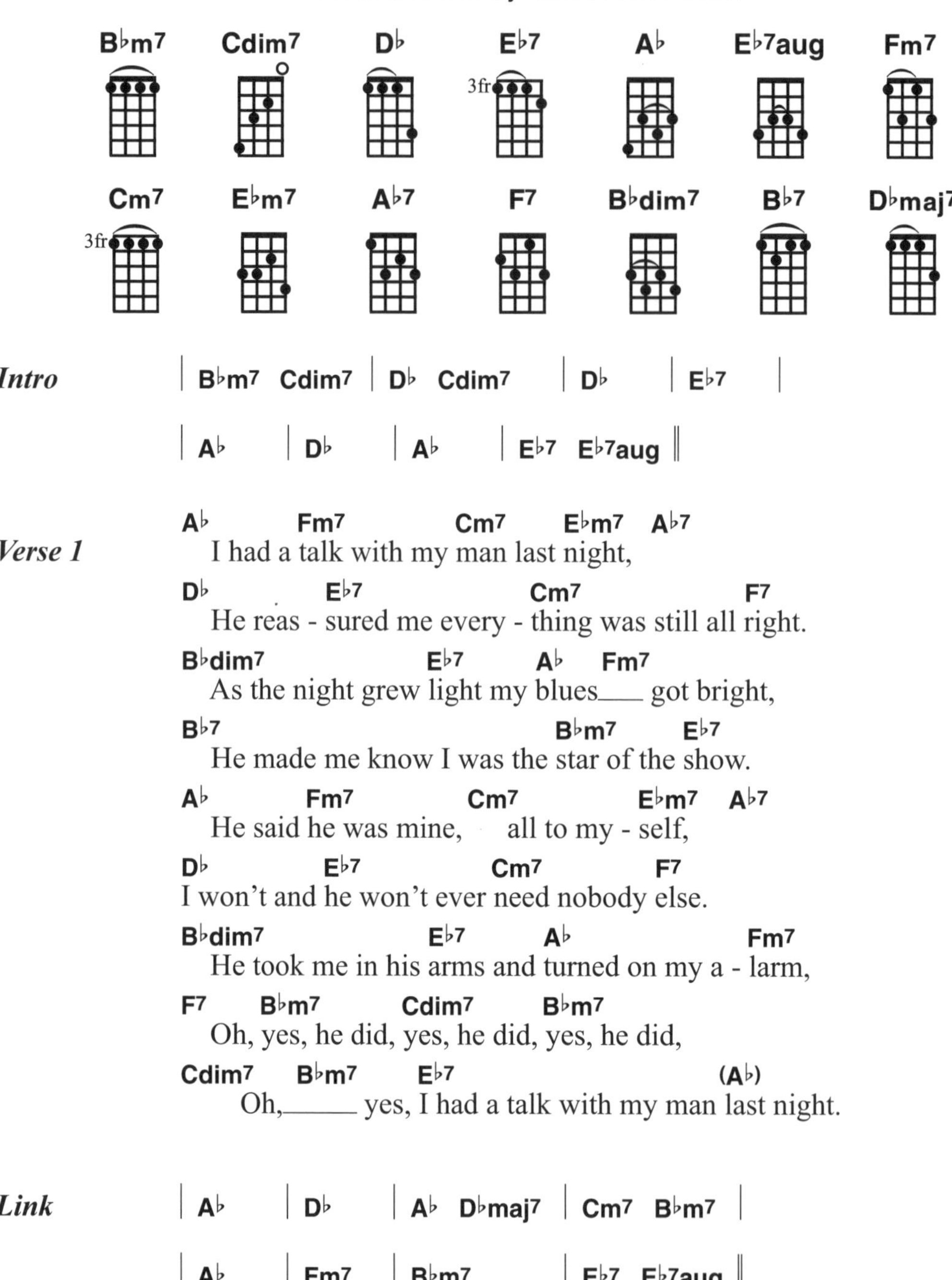

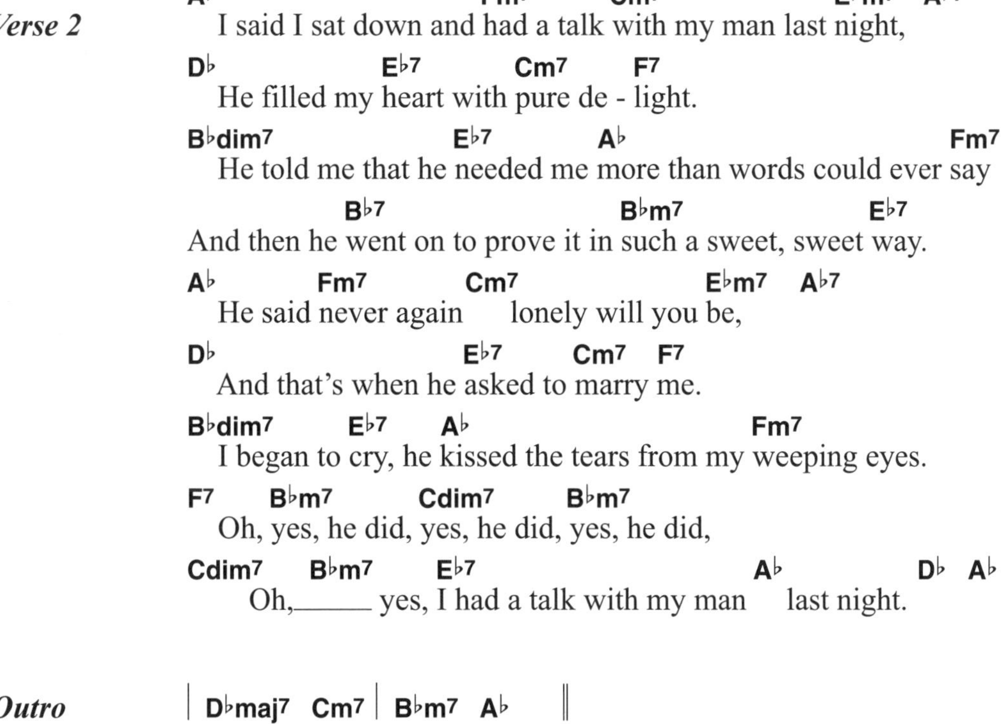
Verse 2
A♭ Fm7 Cm7 E♭m7 A♭7
I said I sat down and had a talk with my man last night,
D♭ E♭7 Cm7 F7
He filled my heart with pure de - light.
B♭dim7 E♭7 A♭ Fm7
He told me that he needed me more than words could ever say
B♭7 B♭m7 E♭7
And then he went on to prove it in such a sweet, sweet way.
A♭ Fm7 Cm7 E♭m7 A♭7
He said never again lonely will you be,
D♭ E♭7 Cm7 F7
And that's when he asked to marry me.
B♭dim7 E♭7 A♭ Fm7
I began to cry, he kissed the tears from my weeping eyes.
F7 B♭m7 Cdim7 B♭m7
Oh, yes, he did, yes, he did, yes, he did,
Cdim7 B♭m7 E♭7 A♭ D♭ A♭
Oh,_____ yes, I had a talk with my man last night.
Outro
| D♭maj7 Cm7 | B♭m7 A♭ ||

I Wish I Knew How It Would Feel To Be Free

Words by Billy Taylor & Dick Dallas
Music by Billy Taylor

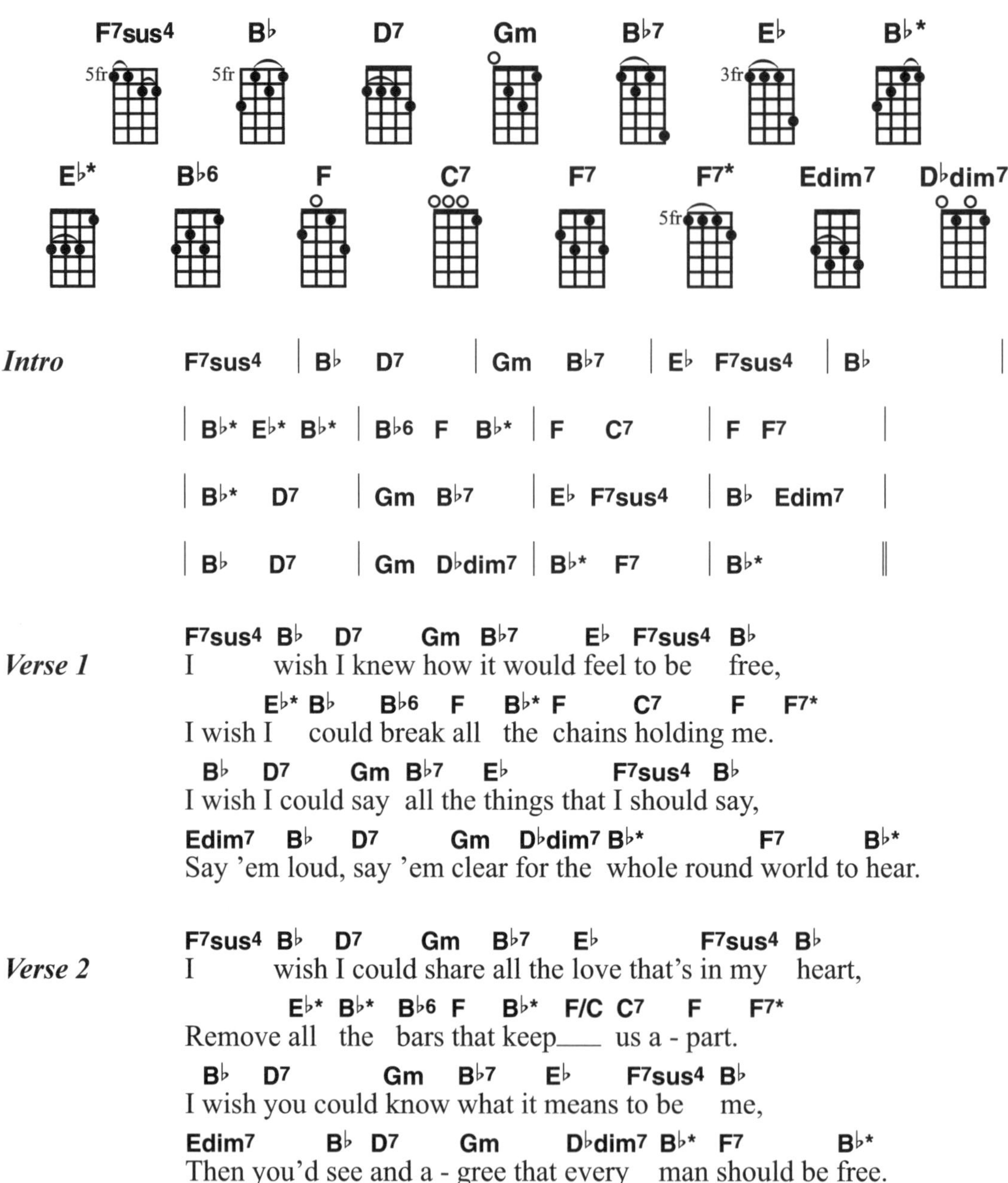

Intro

| F7sus4 | B♭ D7 | Gm B♭7 | E♭ F7sus4 | B♭ |

| B♭* E♭* B♭* | B♭6 F B♭* | F C7 | F F7 |

| B♭* D7 | Gm B♭7 | E♭ F7sus4 | B♭ Edim7 |

| B♭ D7 | Gm D♭dim7 | B♭* F7 | B♭* ||

Verse 1

```
F7sus4  B♭   D7      Gm   B♭7       E♭  F7sus4  B♭
I       wish I knew how it would feel to be     free,
        E♭* B♭     B♭6    F    B♭* F       C7      F    F7*
I wish I    could break all   the  chains holding me.
  B♭    D7       Gm  B♭7      E♭           F7sus4  B♭
I wish I could say   all the things that I should say,
Edim7    B♭      D7        Gm       D♭dim7 B♭*            F7          B♭*
Say 'em loud, say 'em clear for the  whole round world to hear.
```

Verse 2

```
F7sus4  B♭   D7        Gm      B♭7       E♭           F7sus4  B♭
I       wish I could share all the love that's in my      heart,
             E♭*  B♭*  B♭6 F    B♭*   F/C C7     F     F7*
Remove all    the   bars that keep___    us a - part.
  B♭    D7          Gm       B♭7       E♭      F7sus4  B♭
I wish you could know what it means to be      me,
Edim7           B♭   D7       Gm          D♭dim7 B♭*  F7          B♭*
Then you'd see and a - gree that every      man should be free.
```

Verse 3

F7sus4 B♭ D7 Gm B♭7 E♭ F7sus4 B♭
I wish I could give all I'm long - ing to give,

E♭* B♭ B♭6 F B♭* F C7 F F7*
I wish I could live like I'm long - ing to live.

B♭ D7 Gm B♭7 E♭ F7sus4 B♭
I wish I could do all the things that I can do,

Edim7 B♭ D7 Gm D♭dim7 B♭ F7 B♭*
Though I'm way over - due, I'd be start - ing a - new.

Verse 4

F7sus4 B♭ D7 Gm B♭7 E♭ F7sus4 B♭
Well, I wish I could be like a bird in the sky,

E♭* B♭* B♭6 F B♭* F C7 F F7*
How sweet it would be if I found I could fly.

B♭ D7 Gm B♭7 E♭ F7sus4 B♭
I'd soar to the sun and look down at the sea,

Edim7 B♭ D7 Gm
Then I'd sing 'cause I'd know, yeah,

Edim7 B♭ D7 Gm
Then I'd sing 'cause I'd know, yeah,

Edim7 B♭ D7 Gm
Then I'd sing 'cause I'd know,

Edim7 B♭
I'd know how it feels,

D7 Gm Edim7 B♭ D7 Gm
I'd know how it feels to be free, yeah, yeah.

Edim7 B♭ D7 Gm
I'd know how it feels,

Edim7 B♭ D7 Gm Edim7 B♭ D7 Gm Edim7 B♭
Yes, I'd know, I'd know how it feels,

D7 Gm Edim7 B♭ D7 Gm
How it feels to be free. *Ad lib. to fade*

The 'In' Crowd

Words & Music by Billy Page

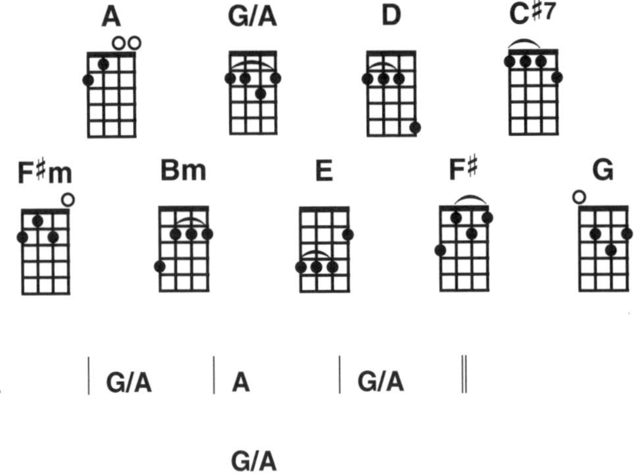

Intro | A | G/A | A | G/A ||

Chorus 1

A G/A
I'm in with the 'In' crowd,
A G/A
I go where the 'In' crowd go,
A G/A
I'm in with the 'In' crowd,
A G/A
And I know what the 'In' crowd know.

Verse 1

D
Anytime of the year don't you hear?
A
Dressin' fine, makin' time,
C♯7
We breeze up and down the street
F♯m
We get respect from the people we meet,
Bm
They make way day or night,
E F♯ G
They know the 'In' crowd is out of sight.

Chorus 2

A G/A
I'm in with the 'In' crowd,
A G/A
I know every latest dance,

```
          A                               G/A
cont.        When you're in with the 'In'    crowd
          A                 G/A
             It's easy to find romance.

          D
Verse 2      At a spa, grab a beat it's really hot,
          A
             If it's square, we ain't there.
          C♯7
             We make every minute count, yeah,
          F♯m
             Our share is always the biggest amount.
          Bm
             Other guys imitate us,
          E                            F♯  G
             But the originals still the greatest, yeah!

          A (G/A)                           A
Link              We got our own way of walkin'
          A (G/A)                           A
                  We got our own way of talkin' yeah.

          D
Verse 3      Any time of the year don't you hear?
          A
             Spendin' cash, talkin' trash.
          C♯7
             Girl I'll show you a real good time,
          F♯m
             Come home with me and leave your troubles behind,
          Bm
             I don't care where you been,
          E                                        F♯    G
             You ain't been nowhere till you've been in,

                             A         G/A
Outro     With the 'In'    crowd, yeah,
                               A
          Oh with the 'In'    crowd,
          G/A                               A
             We got our own way of walkin' yeah,
          G/A                               A
             We got our own way of talkin' yeah,
          G/A                         A  G/A  A
             In the 'In' crowd.                 Fade out
```

Just The Two Of Us

Words & Music by Ralph MacDonald, William Salter & Bill Withers

Intro

| D♭maj7 C7 | Fm7 E♭m7 A♭7 | D♭maj7 C7 | Fm7 |

| D♭maj7 C7(♯5) | Fm7 E♭m7 A♭7 | D♭maj7 C7(♯5) | Fm7 |

Verse 1

D♭maj7 C7 Fm7 E♭m7 A♭7 D♭maj7
I see the crystal raindrops fall and the beauty of it all,
C7 Fm7
Is when the sun comes shining through.
D♭maj7 C7 Fm7 E♭m7 A♭7 D♭maj7
To make those rainbows in my mind when I think of you sometime
C7 Fm7
And I want to spend some time with you.

Chorus 1

D♭maj7
Just the two of us,
C7 Fm7 Em7 E♭m7
We can make it if we try.
A♭7 D♭maj7 C7 Fm7
Just the two of us (just the two of us.)
D♭maj7
Just the two of us,
C7 Fm7 Em7 E♭m7
Building castles in the sky,
A♭7 D♭maj7 C7 Fm7
Just the two of us, you and I.

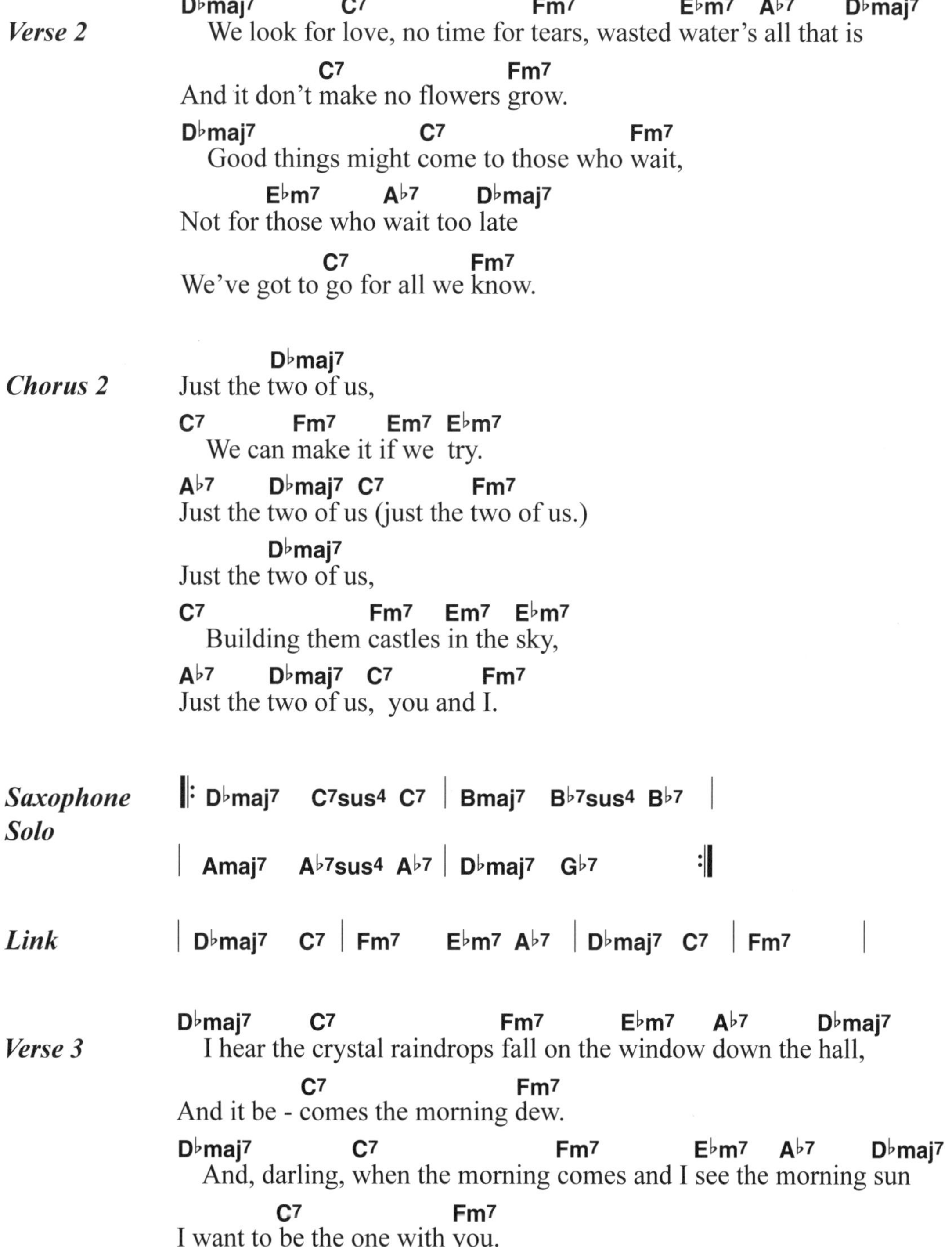

Verse 2

D♭maj7 C7 Fm7 E♭m7 A♭7 D♭maj7
We look for love, no time for tears, wasted water's all that is

C7 Fm7
And it don't make no flowers grow.

D♭maj7 C7 Fm7
Good things might come to those who wait,

E♭m7 A♭7 D♭maj7
Not for those who wait too late

C7 Fm7
We've got to go for all we know.

Chorus 2

D♭maj7
Just the two of us,

C7 Fm7 Em7 E♭m7
We can make it if we try.

A♭7 D♭maj7 C7 Fm7
Just the two of us (just the two of us.)

D♭maj7
Just the two of us,

C7 Fm7 Em7 E♭m7
Building them castles in the sky,

A♭7 D♭maj7 C7 Fm7
Just the two of us, you and I.

Saxophone Solo

‖: D♭maj7 C7sus4 C7 | Bmaj7 B♭7sus4 B♭7 |

| Amaj7 A♭7sus4 A♭7 | D♭maj7 G♭7 :‖

Link

| D♭maj7 C7 | Fm7 E♭m7 A♭7 | D♭maj7 C7 | Fm7 |

Verse 3

D♭maj7 C7 Fm7 E♭m7 A♭7 D♭maj7
I hear the crystal raindrops fall on the window down the hall,

C7 Fm7
And it be - comes the morning dew.

D♭maj7 C7 Fm7 E♭m7 A♭7 D♭maj7
And, darling, when the morning comes and I see the morning sun

C7 Fm7
I want to be the one with you.

```
                 D♭maj7
Chorus 3    Just the two of us,

            C7            Fm7      Em7  E♭m7
               We can make it if we try.

            A♭7      D♭maj7  C7           Fm7
            Just the two of us   (just the two of us.)

                 D♭maj7
            Just the two of us,

            C7                  Fm7     Em7     E♭m7
               Building big castles way on high,

            A♭7      D♭maj7  C7           Fm7
            Just the two of us,   you and I.

                  D♭maj7
Chorus 4    ||: (Just the two of us,)

            C7(♯5)         Fm7           Em7    E♭m7
            Yeah, just the two of us. (We can make it,

            A♭7     D♭maj7             C7(♯5)          Fm7
            Just the two of us.) Just get it together, baby, yeah.

                    D♭maj7     C7(♯5)       Fm7         Em7     E♭m7
            (Just the two of us,)   Just the two of us. (We can make it,

            A♭7     D♭maj7  C7(♯5)  Fm7
            Just the two of us.)              :||  Repeat to fade w/ad lib. sax.
```

Let's Groove

Words & Music by Maurice White & Wayne Vaughn

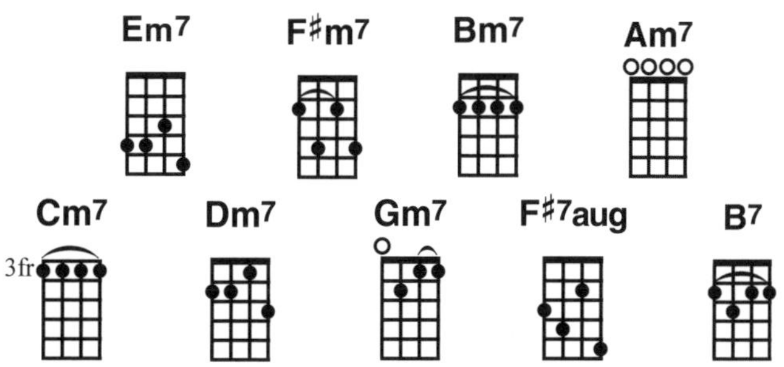


```
Intro       |: Em7        | F♯m7  Bm7 | Em7        | F♯m7  Bm7 :|

            (B7)  Em7                 F♯m7   Bm7
            Let's groove tonight,
                        Em7            F♯m7   Bm7
            Share the spice of life.
                    Em7              F♯m7   Bm7
            Baby, slice it right,
                           Em7                 F♯m7   Bm7
            We're gonna groove tonight.

            Em7                     F♯m7         Bm7
Chorus 1       Let this groove get you to move,
                    Em7                  F♯m7  Bm7
            It's all right, (all right), all      right.
            Em7                     F♯m7          Bm7
               Let this groove set in your shoes,
                          Em7              F♯m7  Bm7
            So stand up, all right, all       right.
```

Verse 1

```
Em7                    F♯m7            Bm7
   Gonna tell you what you can do
           Em7  F♯m7  Bm7
With my love,  all     right.
Em7                         F♯m7              Bm7
   Let you know girl, you're lookin' good,
                Em7   F♯m7  Bm7
You're out of sight, all     right.
     Em7            F♯m7    Bm7
Just move your - self
     Em7            F♯m7          Bm7
And glide like a seven-forty-seven.
     Em7            F♯m7  Bm7         Em7
And lose your - self            in the sky
              F♯m7           Bm7
Among the clouds in the heaven.
```

Chorus 2

```
Em7                    F♯m7            Bm7
   Let this groove light up your fuse,
       Em7                F♯m7  Bm7
It's all right, (all right), all     right.
Em7                     F♯m7          Bm7
   Let this groove, set in your shoes,
          Em7             F♯m7  Bm7
So stand up, all right, all     right.
```

Verse 2

```
Em7                    F♯m7            Bm7
   Let me tell you what you can do
          Em7   F♯m7  Bm7
With my love,  all     right.
Em7                         F♯m7              Bm7
Gotta let you know girl you're lookin' good,
                Em7   F♯m7  Bm7
You're out of sight, all     right.
     Em7    F♯m7   Bm7
Just tell the D. J.
   Em7        F♯m7      Bm7
To play your favourite tune.
           Em7        F♯m7     Bm7
Then you know it's okay,
            Em7      F♯m7         Bm7
What you found is happening now.
```

Chorus 3 As Chorus 2

Chorus 4 As Chorus 1

```
              Am7            Bm7                   Em7
Middle          You will find peace of mind on the floor, take a little time,
              Am7                          Bm7          Em7
                Come and see, you and me give a little sign.
              Cm7                    Dm7          Gm7       F#7aug
                I'll be there after a while if you want my love.
                    B7          Em7   F#m7
              We can boogie on down, down.
              Bm7         Em7   F#m7
              Boogie on down, down.
              Bm7         Em7   F#m7
              Boogie on down, down.
                 Bm7         Em7        F#m7    Bm7
              We boogie on down, on down.

              (Bm7) Em7                F#m7  Bm7
Bridge        Let's  groove tonight,
                       Em7                F#m7  Bm7
              Share the spice of life.
                   Em7               F#m7  Bm7
              Baby slice it right,
                        Em7                F#m7  Bm7
              We're gonna groove tonight.
```

Instrumental 𝄆 Em7 | F#m7 Bm7 | Em7 | F#m7 Bm7 𝄇 *Play 4 times*

```
              Em7               F#m7          Bm7
Chorus 5        Let this groove light up your fuse,
                    Em7              F#m7  Bm7
              It's all  right, (all right), all    right.
              Em7               F#m7         Bm7
                Let this groove set in your shoes
                    Em7             F#m7  Bm7
              Stand up, all right, all     right.  To fade
```

Lady Day And John Coltrane

Words & Music by Gil Scott-Heron

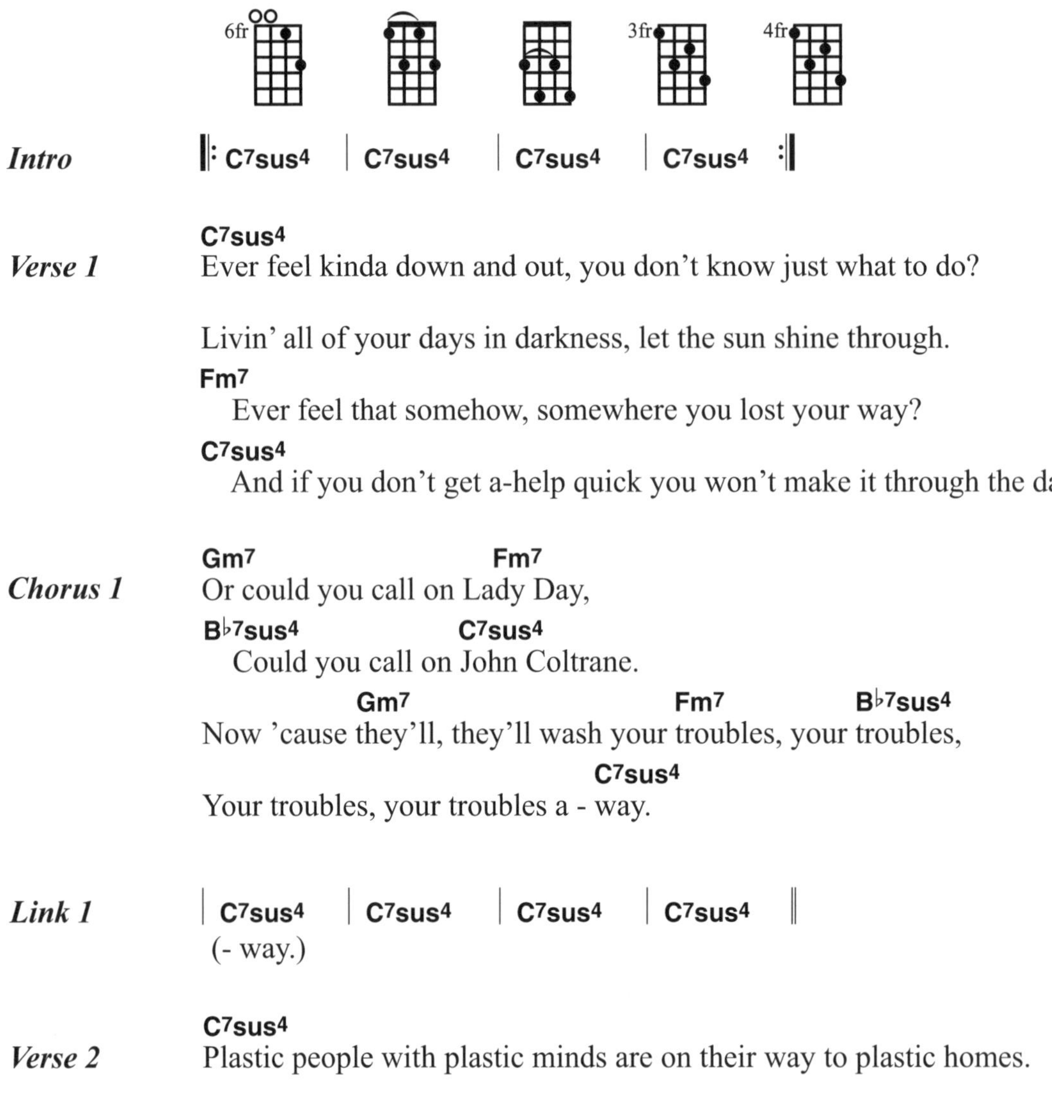

Intro 𝄆 C7sus4 | C7sus4 | C7sus4 | C7sus4 𝄇

Verse 1

C7sus4
Ever feel kinda down and out, you don't know just what to do?

Livin' all of your days in darkness, let the sun shine through.

Fm7
Ever feel that somehow, somewhere you lost your way?

C7sus4
And if you don't get a-help quick you won't make it through the day.

Chorus 1

Gm7 Fm7
Or could you call on Lady Day,

B♭7sus4 C7sus4
Could you call on John Coltrane.

Gm7 Fm7 B♭7sus4
Now 'cause they'll, they'll wash your troubles, your troubles,

C7sus4
Your troubles, your troubles a - way.

Link 1 | C7sus4 | C7sus4 | C7sus4 | C7sus4 ||
(- way.)

Verse 2

C7sus4
Plastic people with plastic minds are on their way to plastic homes.

No beginning, there ain't no ending just on and on and on and on and on.

Fm7
It's all because they're so afraid to say that they're alone.

C7sus4
Until I hear old Rodney ridin' on his saxophone.

Chorus 2 As Chorus 1

Keyboard solo

| C7sus4 (- way.) | C7sus4 | C7sus4 | C7sus4 ‖
: C7sus4	C7sus4	C7sus4	C7sus4 :
Fm7	Fm7	Fm7	Fm7
C7sus4	C7sus4	C7sus4	C7sus4
Gm7	Fm7	B♭7sus4	C7sus4
Gm7	Fm7	B♭7sus4	B♭7sus4
C7sus4	C7sus4	C7sus4 All right.	C7sus4 ‖

Verse 3 As Verse 1

Chorus 3

```
Gm7                   Fm7
Or could you call on Lady Day,
B♭7sus4            C7sus4
   Could you call on John Coltrane.
                         Gm7             Fm7
Now 'cause they'll, they'll wash your troubles,
      B♭7sus4
Your troubles, your troubles, your troubles,
B7sus4
   Your troubles, your troubles, your troubles,
B♭7sus4                                          C7sus4
   Your troubles, your troubles, your troubles a - way.
```

Outro

```
C7sus4
They'll wash your troubles away
```

They'll wash your troubles away

Your troubles, your troubles, your troubles, your troubles away

Yeah, they'll wash your troubles away

They'll wash your troubles away

Yeah, yeah, yeah, yeah, yeah. *To fade*

Let's Stay Together

Words & Music by Al Green, Willie Mitchell & Al Jackson

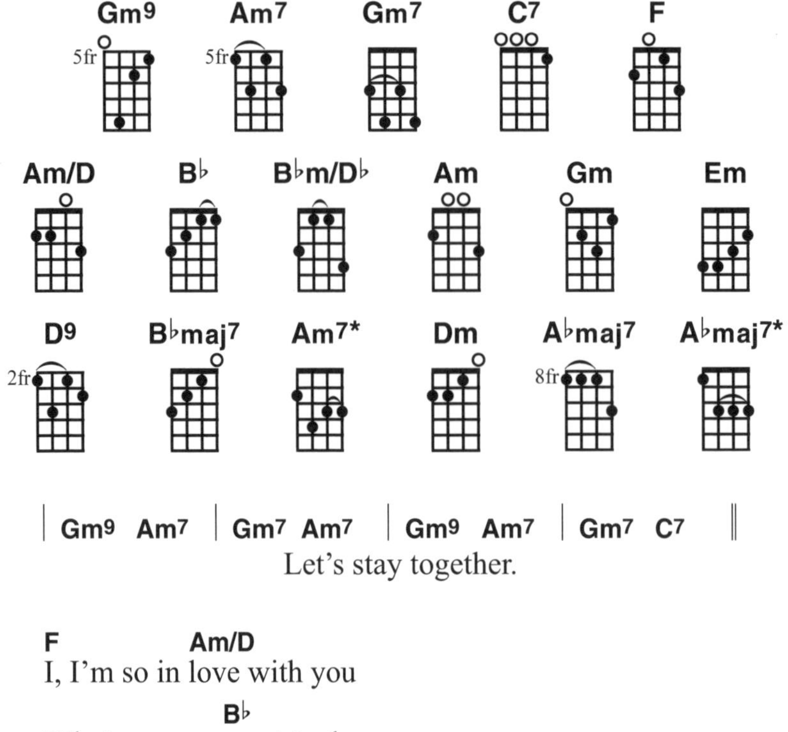

Intro

| Gm9 Am7 | Gm7 Am7 | Gm9 Am7 | Gm7 C7 ||
Let's stay together.

Verse 1

F Am/D
I, I'm so in love with you
B♭
Whatever you want to do
B♭m/D♭
Is all right with me.
Am Gm F Em D9
'Cause you___ make me feel so brand new,
Am Gm F Am D9
And I______ want to spend my life with you.

Verse 2

F Am/D
Let me say, since baby, since we've been to - gether
B♭
Ooh, loving you for - ever
B♭m/D♭
Is what I need
Am Gm F Em D9
Let me be the one you come running to
Am Gm F Am D9
I'll never be un - true.

Chorus 1

Gm9 Am7*
Ooh baby, let's, let's stay to - gether

Gm7
Lovin' you whether, whether

B♭maj7 Am7* Dm C7
Times are good or bad, happy or sad.

Link 1

| Gm9 | Gm9 | A♭maj7 | Gm9 | A♭maj7* | A♭maj7* ||

B♭maj7 Am7* Dm C7
Whether times are good or bad, happy or sad.

Verse 3

F Am/D
Why somebody, why people break up

B♭
Oh, and turn around and make up

B♭m/D♭
I just can't see____

Am Gm F Em D9
You'd_____ never do that to me (would you, baby)

Am Gm F Am D9
Staying__ around you is all I see

(Here's what I want us to do)

Chorus 3

Gm(9) Am7*
Let's, we oughta stay to - gether

Gm7
Loving you whether, whether

B♭maj7 Am7* Dm C7
Times are good or bad, happy or sad

Gm9 Am7
Come on, let's, let's stay to - gether

Gm7
Loving you whether, whether

B♭maj7 Am7* Dm C7
Times are good or bad, happy or sad

B♭maj7 Am7* Gm7 C7
'Cause you're meant for me, I can't set you free, woman.

Gm9 Am7*
Outro chorus ||: Let's, oh girl, let's stay to - gether

Gm7
Loving you whether, whether

B♭maj7 Am7* Gm7 C7
Times are good or bad, happy or sad

B♭maj7 Am7* Gm7 C7
'Cause you're out with me, you can't set me free, woman. :||

Repeat with ad lib. vocal to fade

Midnight At The Oasis

Words & Music by David Nichtern

E/F♯ (4fr)   A/B   B/C♯ (6fr)   F♯/G♯   G♯/A♯   D♯maj7   G♯   C♯9 (5fr)

F♯ (4fr)   B9 (3fr)   Emaj7 (4fr)   F♯6 (6fr)   A♯9   G/G♯ (2fr)   D♯   D♯7

Intro | E/F♯ A/B B/C♯ | F♯/G♯ G♯/A♯ |

Verse 1

```
D♯maj7                 G♯   C♯9
   Midnight at the oa - sis,
D♯maj7                     G♯   C♯9
   Send your camel to bed.
D♯maj7                        G♯   C♯9
   Shadows painting our fac - es,
F♯   B9   F♯/G♯          G♯/A♯
Traces of romance in our heads.
D♯maj7                     G♯   C♯9
   Heaven's holding a half-moon,
D♯maj7                 G♯   C♯9
   Shining just for us.
D♯maj7                   G♯    C♯9    F♯   B9
   Let's slip off to a sand dune, real soon,
F♯/G♯                    G♯/A♯
And kick up a little dust.
```

Chorus 1

```
Emaj7  F♯6  A/B          B/C♯
Come   on,  Cactus is our friend,
Emaj7  F♯6              A/B   B/C♯
He'll  point out the way.
Emaj7  F♯6  A/B                B/C♯
Come   on,  till the evening ends,
F♯/G♯                 A♯9
Till the evening ends.
```

Verse 2

```
D♯maj7            G♯   C♯9
   You don't have to answer,
D♯maj7             G♯       C♯9
   There's no need to speak.
D♯maj7               G♯   C♯9 F♯   B9
   I'll be your belly dancer,   prancer,
    F♯/G♯           G♯/A♯
And you can be my sheik.
```

Guitar Solo

```
                        Play 3 times
|: D♯maj7        | G♯     C♯9   :|| F♯     B9    | F♯/G♯   G♯/A♯ |

                        Play 3 times
|: Emaj7   F♯6   | A/B    B/C♯  :|| F♯/G♯  A♯9   |
```

Verse 3

```
D♯maj7                       G♯ C♯9
   I know your Daddy's a sultan,
D♯maj7                G♯    C♯9
   A nomad known to all.
D♯maj7                G♯    C♯9           F♯    B9
   With fifty girls to attend him, they all send him,
F♯/G♯               G♯/A♯
Jump at his beck and call.
D♯maj7                 G♯         C♯9
   But you won't need no harem honey,
D♯maj7           G♯          C♯9
   When I'm by your side.
D♯maj7                     G♯   C♯9  F♯   B9
   And you won't need no camel,    no,  no,
        F♯/G♯           A♯9
When I take you for a ride.
```

Chorus 2

```
Emaj7 F♯6 A/B          B/C♯
Come  on, Cactus is our friend,
Emaj7 F♯6          A/B  B/C♯
He'll point out the way.
Emaj7 F♯6 A/B              B/C♯
Come  on, till the evening ends,
F♯/G♯              A♯9
Till the evening ends.
```

Verse 4

```
D#maj7                G#   C#9
   Midnight at the oa - sis,
D#maj7                    G#   C#9
   Send your camel to bed.
D#maj7                          G#    C#9
   Got shadows painting our fac - es,
     F#  B9   F#/G#             G#/A#
And traces of romance in our heads.
```

Outro ‖: G# G/G# | D# D#7 :‖ *Repeat to fade*

Lovin' You

Words & Music by Minnie Riperton & Richard Rudolph

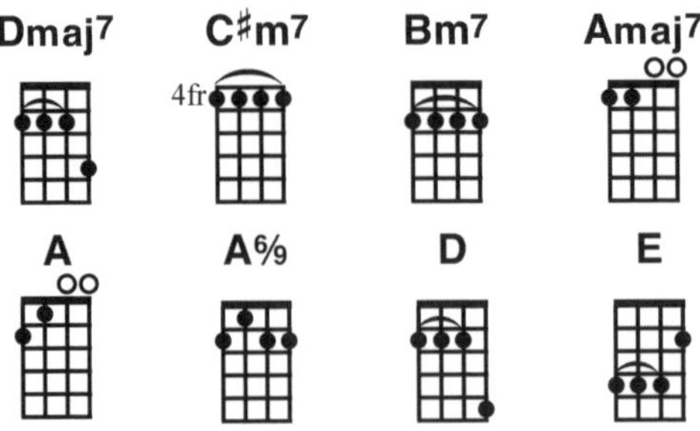

Intro

```
|: Dmaj7   C♯m7   | Bm7   Amaj7   :|
```

Verse 1

```
Dmaj7 C♯m7  Bm7                  Amaj7
Lovin' you is easy 'cause  you're beautiful
Dmaj7                  C♯m7    Bm7          Amaj7
   Makin' love with you, is all I wanna do.
Dmaj7     C♯m7  Bm7                  Amaj7
   Lovin' you is more than just a dream come true
Dmaj7                           C♯m7 Bm7           Amaj7
   And everything that I do, is out of lovin' you.
```

Chorus 1

```
Dmaj7          C♯m7
La la la la la, la la la la la
Bm7              Amaj7
La la la la la la la la la la la
Dmaj7             C♯m7
   Do do do do do
Bm7                        Amaj7
Ah - ah - ah -ah - ah - ah.
```

Bridge 1

```
Bm7                C♯m7
No one else can make me feel
      Bm7    C♯m7     A     A6/9
The colours that you bring.
Bm7                    C♯m7
Stay with me while we grow old
       Bm7    C♯m7      D       E
And we will live each day in springtime,
```

Verse 2

Dmaj7 C♯m7 Bm7 Amaj7
'Cause lovin' you has made my life so beautiful

Dmaj7 C♯m7 Bm7 Amaj7
And every day of my life is filled with lovin' you.

Dmaj7 C♯m7 Bm7 Amaj7
Lovin' you I see your soul come shinin' through

Dmaj7 C♯m7 Bm7 Amaj7
And every time that we oooh, I'm more in love with you.

Chorus 2

Dmaj7 C♯m7
La la la la la, la la la la la

Bm7 Amaj7
La la la la la la la la la la la

Dmaj7 C♯m7
Do do do do do

Bm7 Amaj7
Ah - ah - ah -ah - ah - ah.

Bridge 2

Bm7 C♯m7
No one else can make me feel

Bm7 C♯m7 A A6/9
The colours that you bring.

Bm7 C♯m7
Stay with me while we grow old

Bm7 C♯m7 D E
And we will live each day in springtime,

Verse 3

Dmaj7 C♯m7 Bm7 Amaj7
'Cause lovin' you is easy 'cause you're beautiful

Dmaj7 C♯m7 Bm7 Amaj7
And every day of my life is filled with lovin' you.

Dmaj7 C♯m7 Bm7 Amaj7
Lovin' you I see your soul come shinin' through

Dmaj7 C♯m7 Bm7 Amaj7
And every time that we oooh, I'm more in love with you.

Chorus 3

Dmaj7 C♯m7
La la la la la, la la la la la

Bm7 Amaj7
La la la la la la la la la la la

Dmaj7 C♯m7
Do do do do do

Bm7 Amaj7
Ah - ah - ah -ah - ah - ah.

Outro ‖: Dmaj7 C♯m7 | Bm7 Amaj7 :‖ *ad lib. vocals to fade*

Midnight Train To Georgia

Words & Music by Jim Weatherly

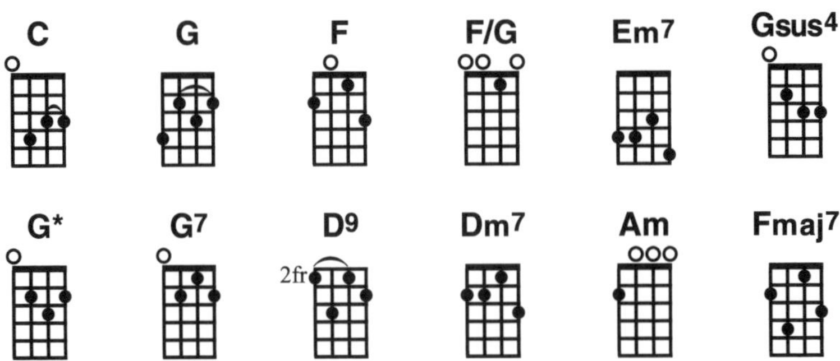

To match original recording, tune ukulele up one semitone

Intro | C G | F F/G | C G | F F/G ||

Verse 1

```
C       Em7   F
   L.A.___
Gsus4  G*  C            Em7          F   G*  G7
   Proved    too much for the man,
C      Em7                F
   So he's leavin' the life
D9     F/G                 G*
   He's come to know.
C                 Em7                F   G*  Gsus4
   He said he's goin' back to find
C     Em7                F            G*  G7
Ooh,__ what's left of his world,
C                  Em7         F
   The world he left behind
   D9       F/G     G*
Not so long ago.__
```

Chorus 1

```
        C          Em7
He's leaving
Dm7           G*          Gsus4     C         Em7    Dm7    G*  Gsus4
   On that midnight train    to Georgia,
C                           Em7   Am
Said he's goin' back
D9               F/G                  G
To a simpler place and time, oh yes he is.
```

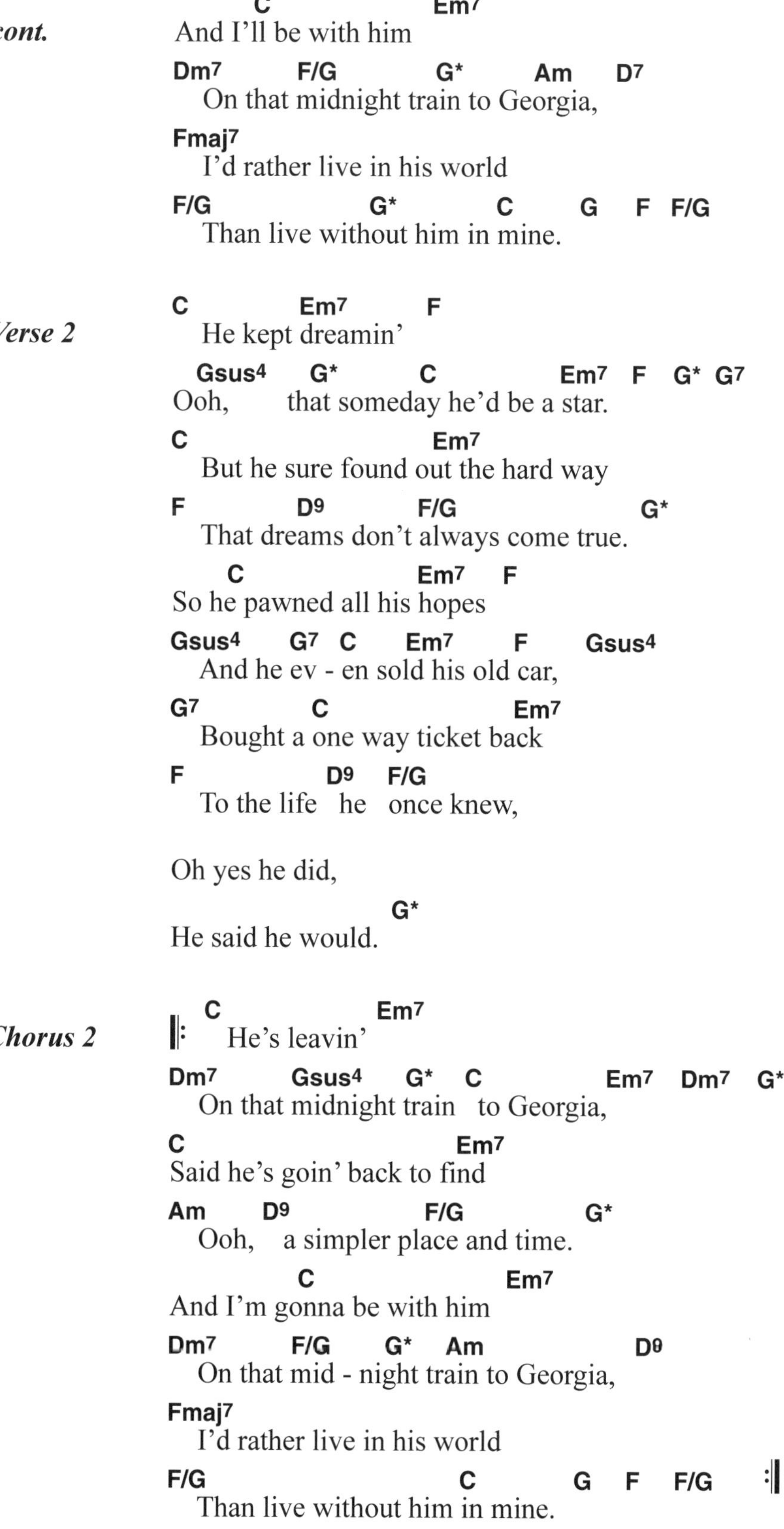

cont.

C Em7
And I'll be with him

Dm7 F/G G* Am D7
On that midnight train to Georgia,

Fmaj7
I'd rather live in his world

F/G G* C G F F/G
Than live without him in mine.

Verse 2

C Em7 F
He kept dreamin'

Gsus4 G* C Em7 F G* G7
Ooh, that someday he'd be a star.

C Em7
But he sure found out the hard way

F D9 F/G G*
That dreams don't always come true.

C Em7 F
So he pawned all his hopes

Gsus4 G7 C Em7 F Gsus4
And he ev - en sold his old car,

G7 C Em7
Bought a one way ticket back

F D9 F/G
To the life he once knew,

Oh yes he did,

G*
He said he would.

Chorus 2

𝄆 C Em7
He's leavin'

Dm7 Gsus4 G* C Em7 Dm7 G*
On that midnight train to Georgia,

C Em7
Said he's goin' back to find

Am D9 F/G G*
Ooh, a simpler place and time.

C Em7
And I'm gonna be with him

Dm7 F/G G* Am D9
On that mid - night train to Georgia,

Fmaj7
I'd rather live in his world

F/G C G F F/G 𝄇
Than live without him in mine.

Repeat to fade with vocal ad lib.

Ordinary Joe

Words & Music by Terrence Callier

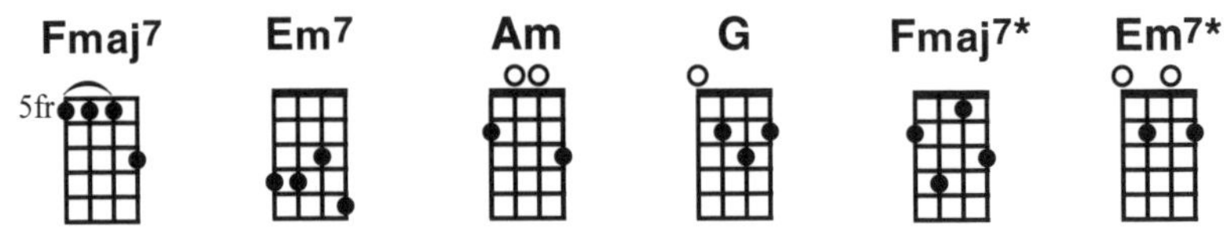

Intro | Fmaj7 | Em7 | Fmaj7 | Em7 :|

Verse 1

(Em7) Fmaj7
For my opening line
Em7
I might try to indicate my state of mind,
Fmaj7
Or turn you on, or tell you that I'm
Em7
Laughing just to keep from crying.
Fmaj7 Em7
Pretty music, when you hear it,
Fmaj7 Em7
Keep on trying to get near it,
Fmaj7 Em7
A little rhythm for your spirit,
Am G Fmaj7* Em7*
But that's what it's for, come on in here's the door.

Chorus 1

Fmaj7 Em7
And I've seen a sparrow get high
Fmaj7* Em7*
And waste his time in the sky.
Fmaj7 Em7
And he thinks it's easy to fly,
Fmaj7* Em7*
He's just a little bit freer than I.

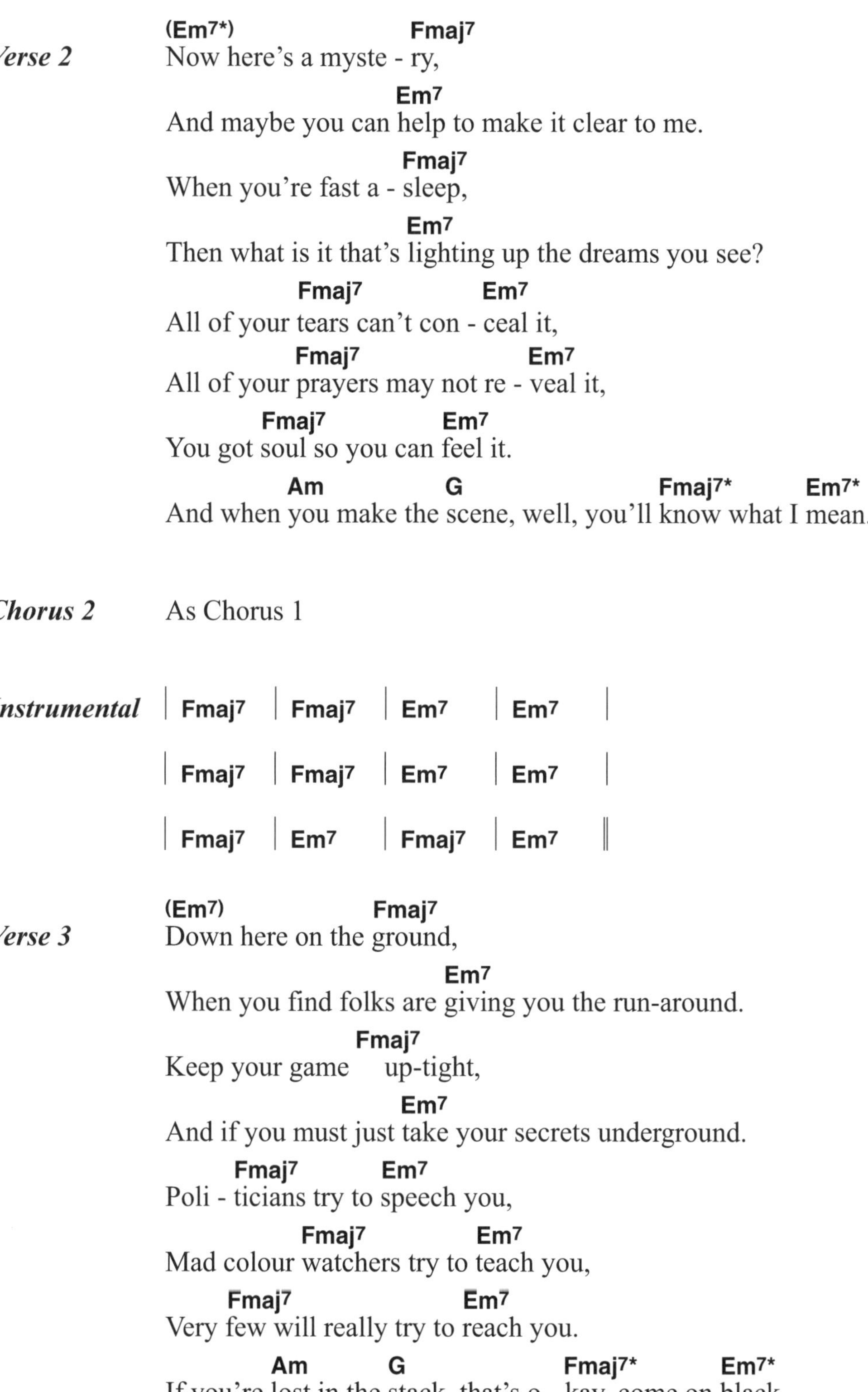

Verse 2

(Em7*) Fmaj7
Now here's a myste - ry,
Em7
And maybe you can help to make it clear to me.
Fmaj7
When you're fast a - sleep,
Em7
Then what is it that's lighting up the dreams you see?
Fmaj7 Em7
All of your tears can't con - ceal it,
Fmaj7 Em7
All of your prayers may not re - veal it,
Fmaj7 Em7
You got soul so you can feel it.
Am G Fmaj7* Em7*
And when you make the scene, well, you'll know what I mean.

Chorus 2

As Chorus 1

Instrumental

Fmaj7	Fmaj7	Em7	Em7
Fmaj7	Fmaj7	Em7	Em7
Fmaj7	Em7	Fmaj7	Em7	

Verse 3

(Em7) Fmaj7
Down here on the ground,
Em7
When you find folks are giving you the run-around.
Fmaj7
Keep your game up-tight,
Em7
And if you must just take your secrets underground.
Fmaj7 Em7
Poli - ticians try to speech you,
Fmaj7 Em7
Mad colour watchers try to teach you,
Fmaj7 Em7
Very few will really try to reach you.
Am G Fmaj7* Em7*
If you're lost in the stack, that's o - kay, come on black.

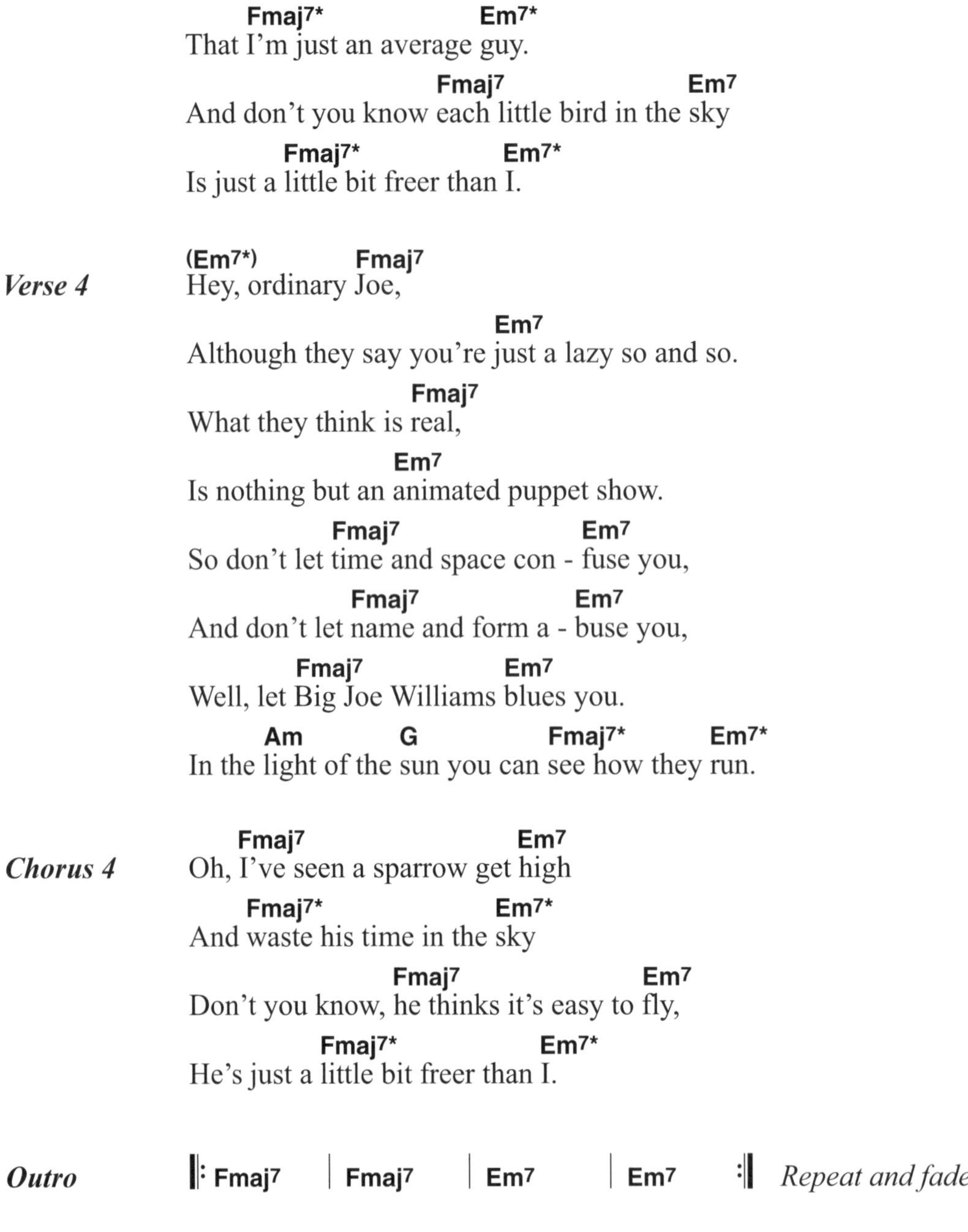

Chorus 3

Fmaj7 Em7
Now I'd be the last to de - ny

Fmaj7* Em7*
That I'm just an average guy.

Fmaj7 Em7
And don't you know each little bird in the sky

Fmaj7* Em7*
Is just a little bit freer than I.

Verse 4

(Em7*) Fmaj7
Hey, ordinary Joe,

Em7
Although they say you're just a lazy so and so.

Fmaj7
What they think is real,

Em7
Is nothing but an animated puppet show.

Fmaj7 Em7
So don't let time and space con - fuse you,

Fmaj7 Em7
And don't let name and form a - buse you,

Fmaj7 Em7
Well, let Big Joe Williams blues you.

Am G Fmaj7* Em7*
In the light of the sun you can see how they run.

Chorus 4

Fmaj7 Em7
Oh, I've seen a sparrow get high

Fmaj7* Em7*
And waste his time in the sky

Fmaj7 Em7
Don't you know, he thinks it's easy to fly,

Fmaj7* Em7*
He's just a little bit freer than I.

Outro

𝄆 Fmaj7 | Fmaj7 | Em7 | Em7 𝄇 *Repeat and fade*

Sir Duke

Words & Music by Stevie Wonder

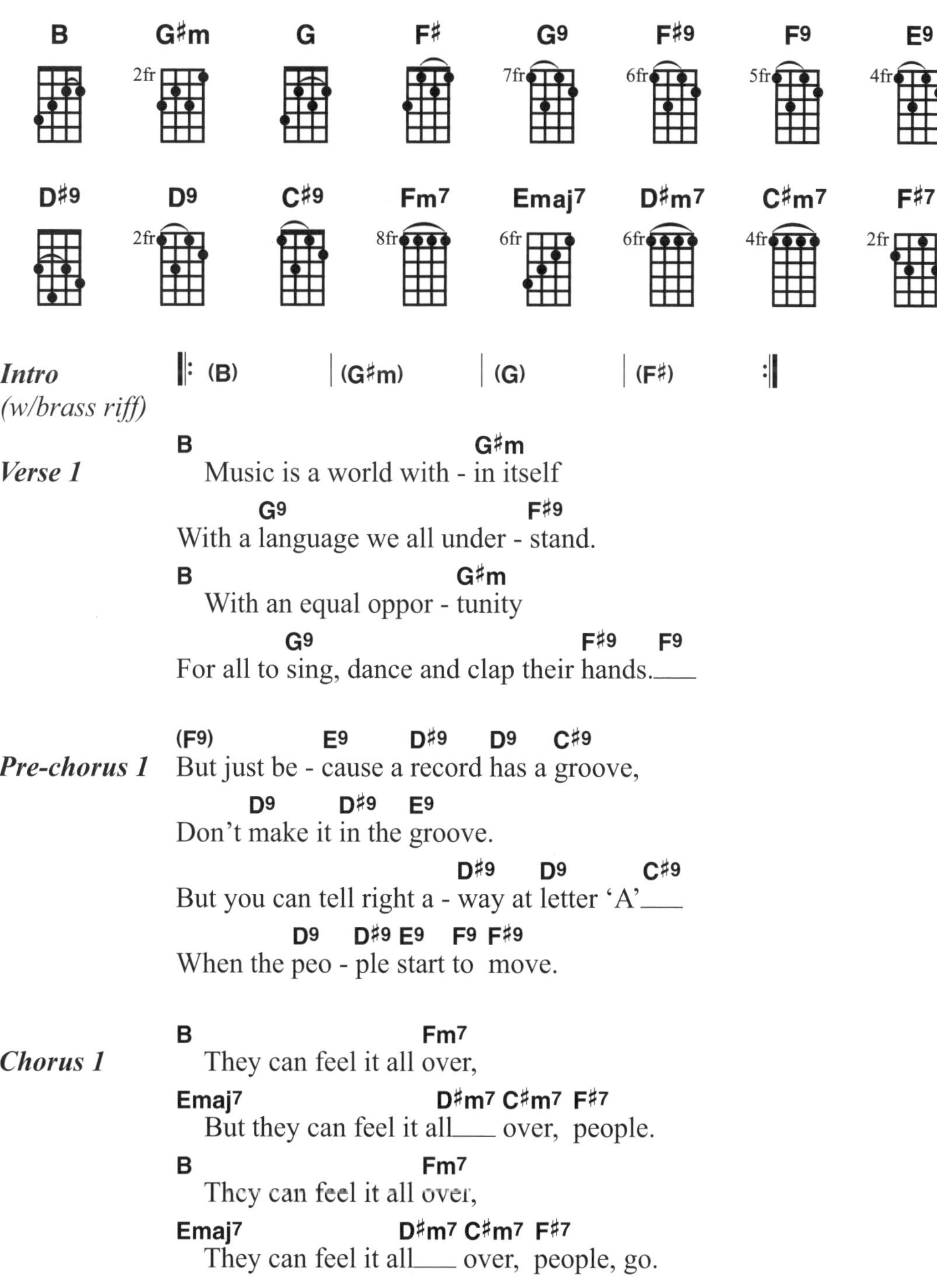

Intro
(w/brass riff)
𝄆 (B) | (G♯m) | (G) | (F♯) 𝄇

Verse 1

B G♯m
Music is a world with - in itself
G9 F♯9
With a language we all under - stand.
B G♯m
With an equal oppor - tunity
G9 F♯9 F9
For all to sing, dance and clap their hands.___

Pre-chorus 1

(F9) E9 D♯9 D9 C♯9
But just be - cause a record has a groove,
D9 D♯9 E9
Don't make it in the groove.
D♯9 D9 C♯9
But you can tell right a - way at letter 'A'___
D9 D♯9 E9 F9 F♯9
When the peo - ple start to move.

Chorus 1

B Fm7
They can feel it all over,
Emaj7 D♯m7 C♯m7 F♯7
But they can feel it all___ over, people.
B Fm7
They can feel it all over,
Emaj7 D♯m7 C♯m7 F♯7
They can feel it all___ over, people, go.

Bridge 1

| N.C.(B) | N.C.(B) | N.C.(B) | N.C.(B) |

| N.C.(B) | N.C.(B) | N.C.(B) | N.C.(B) |

| N.C.(B) | N.C.(B) | N.C.(B) | N.C.(F♯) |

| N.C.(B) | N.C.(B) | N.C.(B) | N.C.(F♯) ||

Verse 2

```
B                         G♯m
   Music knows it is and always will
            G9                         F♯9
Be one of the things that life just won't quit.
B                                  G♯m
   But here are some of music's pioneers
                  G9                F♯9  F9
That time will not allow us to for - get  now.
```

Pre-chorus 2

```
(F9)          E9       D♯9      D9       C♯9
For there's Basie, Miller, Satch - mo
      D9           D♯9    E9
And the king of all, Sir Duke.
                             D♯9    D9       C♯9
And with a voice like Ella's ringing out
                    D9     D♯9  E9    F9      F♯9
There's no way  the  band could lose.
```

Chorus 2

```
B                       Fm7
   You can feel it all over,
Emaj7                  D♯m7 C♯m7  F♯7
   You can feel it all___ over,  people.
B                       Fm7
   You can feel it all over,
Emaj7                  D♯m7 C♯m7  F♯7
   You can feel it all___ over,  people.
```

Chorus 3 As Chorus 2

Bridge 2 As Bridge 1

Chorus 4 As Chorus 2

Chorus 5

```
B                          Fm7
   You can feel it all over,
Emaj7                 D#m7 C#m7  F#7
   You can feel it all___ over,  people.
B                          Fm7
   You can feel it all over,
Emaj7                            D#m7  C#m7             F#7
   I can feel it all over, all        over, all ov - er now people.
```

Chorus 6

```
B                            Fm7
   Can't you feel it all over?
Emaj7                D#m7  C#m7    F#7
   Come on let's feel it all ov - er, people.
B                          Fm7
   You can feel it all over,
Emaj7             D#m7  C#m7  F#7
   Everybody all       over,  people, go.
```

Outro As Bridge 1

Spanish Harlem

Words & Music by Jerry Leiber & Phil Spector

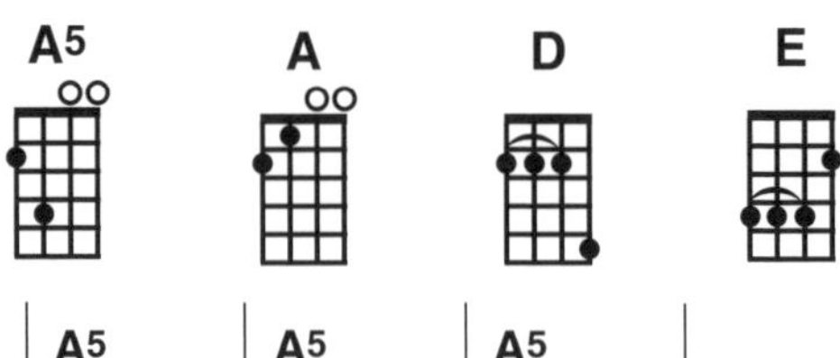

Intro | A5 | A5 | A5 | A5 |

A
La la la, la la la, la la la la.

La la la, la la la, la la la la.

Verse 1

A
There's a rose in black and Spanish Harlem,

A rose in black and Spanish Harlem.

D
It is a special one, it never sees the sun,

It only comes out when the moon is on the run

A
And all the stars are gleaming.

E
It's growing in the street right up through the concrete,

A
But soft, sweet and dreaming.

Verse 2

A
There is a rose in Spanish Harlem,

A rose in black and Spanish Harlem.

D
With eyes as black as coal that look down in his soul,

And start a fire there, and then he loses control,

A
I'm gonna beg his pardon, yeah.

E
He's goin' to pick that rose and watch her as she grows

A
In his garden.

Instrumental	A	A	A	A
	A	A	A	A
	D	D	D	D
	D	A	A	
	E	E	E	E
	A	A	A	A

Verse 3 As Verse 2

Outro

```
              A
𝄆 La la la, la la la, la la la la.
La la, la la la, la la la la. 𝄇  Repeat to fade
```

Strawberry Letter 23

Words & Music by Shuggie Otis

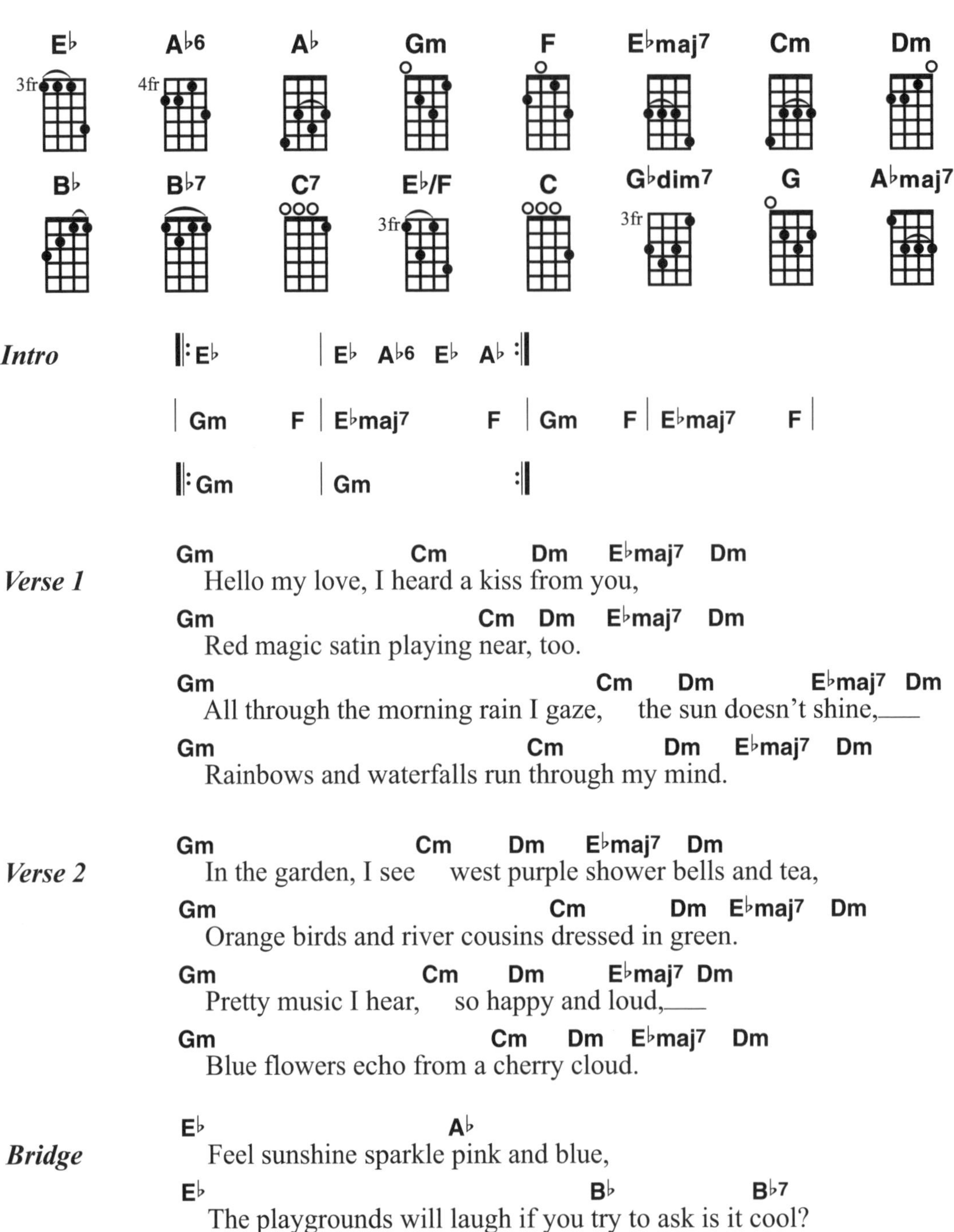

cont.

E♭ C7 F
If you arrive and don't see me I'm going to be with my baby,

E♭/F C E♭/F G♭dim
I am free, flying in her arms over the sea.

Verse 3

Gm Cm Dm E♭maj7 Dm
Stained window yellow candy screen, see speakers of kite,______

Gm Cm Dm E♭maj7 Dm
With velvet roses digging freedom flight.

Gm Cm Dm E♭maj7 Dm
A present from you, straw - berry letter twenty-two,

Gm Cm Dm E♭maj7 Dm
The music plays, I sit in for a few.

Interlude

E♭ A♭6 E♭ A♭ E♭
Ooh, ooh, ooh, ooh, ooh.

A♭6 E♭ A♭ E♭
Ooh, ooh, ooh, ooh, ooh.

A♭6 E♭ A♭ E♭
Ooh, ooh, ooh, ooh, ooh.

A♭6 E♭ A♭
Ooh, ooh, ooh, ooh.

Instrumental

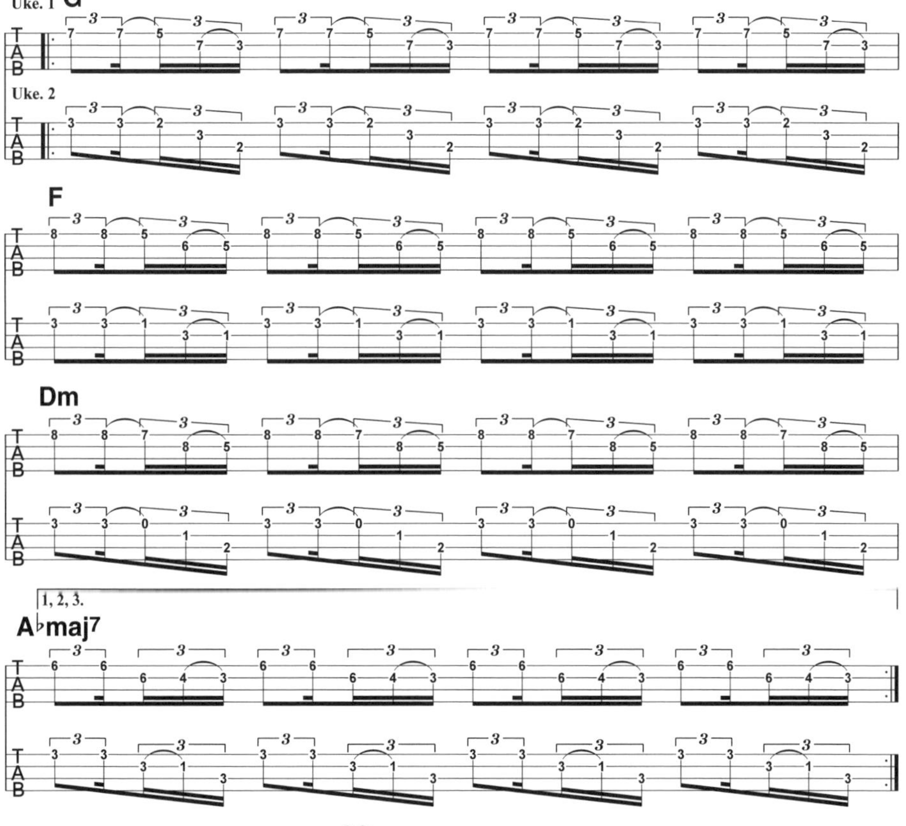

cont.

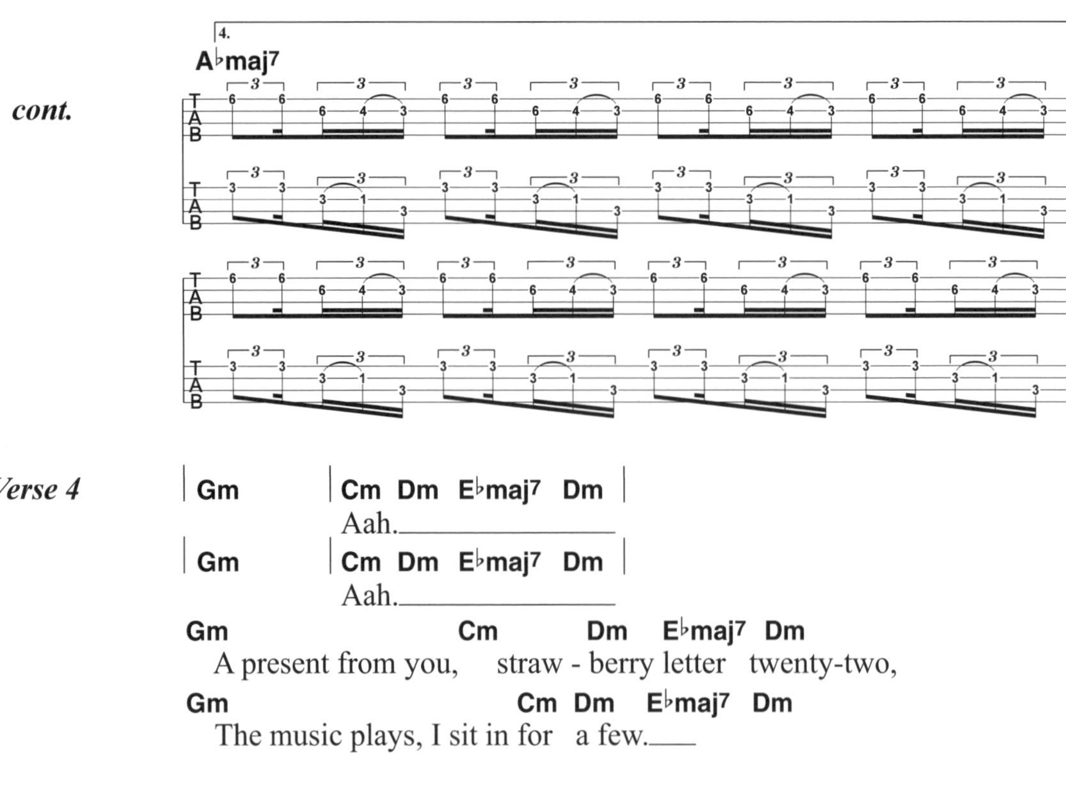

Verse 4

| **Gm** | **Cm Dm E♭maj7 Dm** |
Aah.______

| **Gm** | **Cm Dm E♭maj7 Dm** |
Aah.______

Gm **Cm** **Dm** **E♭maj7** **Dm**
A present from you, straw - berry letter twenty-two,

Gm **Cm** **Dm** **E♭maj7** **Dm**
The music plays, I sit in for a few.___

Outro

𝄆 **E♭** | **E♭ A♭6 E♭ A♭** 𝄇 *Repeat ad lib. to fade*

Sunny

Words & Music by Bobby Hebb

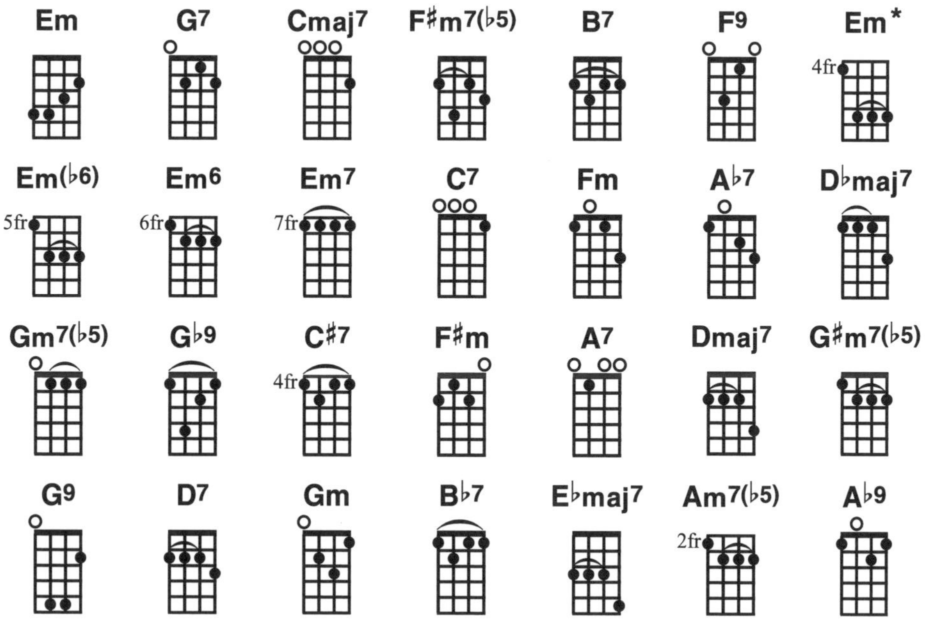
Em
G7
Cmaj7
F♯m7(♭5)
B7
F9
Em*
4fr
Em(♭6)
5fr
Em6
6fr
Em7
7fr
C7
Fm
A♭7
D♭maj7
Gm7(♭5)
G♭9
C♯7
4fr
F♯m
A7
Dmaj7
G♯m7(♭5)
G9
D7
Gm
B♭7
E♭maj7
Am7(♭5)
2fr
A♭9

Verse 1

```
Em        G7                    Cmaj7                  F♯m7(♭5)   B7
Sunny,      yesterday my life was filled with rain.
Em        G7                    Cmaj7                       F♯m7(♭5)   B7
Sunny,      you smiled at me and really eased the pain.
           Em                                  G7
Now the dark days are done and the bright days are here,
Cmaj7                     F9
My sunny one shines so sincere,
F♯m7(♭5)            B7              Em*    Em(♭6)  Em6  Em7
   Sunny, one so true, I love you.
```

Verse 2

Em G7 Cmaj7 F♯m7(♭5) B7
Sunny, thank you for the sunshine bou - quet.

Em G7 Cmaj7 F♯m7(♭5) B7
Sunny, thank you for the love you brought my way.

Em G7
You gave to me your all and all

Cmaj7 F9
And now I feel ten feet tall,

F♯m7(♭5) B7 Em C7
Sunny, one so true, I love you.

Verse 3

Fm A♭7 D♭maj7 Gm7(♭5) C7
Sunny, thank you for the truth you let me see.

Fm A♭7 D♭maj7 Gm7(♭5) C7
Sunny, thank you for the facts from A to Zee.

Fm A♭7
My life was torn like a wind-blown sand,

D♭maj7 G♭9
Then a rock was formed when you held my hand.

Gm7(♭5) C7 Fm C♯7
Sunny, one so true, I love you.

Verse 4

F♯m A7 Dmaj7 G♯m7(♭5) C♯7
Sunny, thank you for the smile upon your face.

F♯m A7 Dmaj7 G♯m7(♭5) C♯7
Sunny, thank you, thank you for that gleam that flows with grace.

F♯m A7
You're my spark of nature's fire,

Dmaj7 G9
You're my sweet com - plete desire,

G♯m7(♭5) C♯7 F♯m D7
Sunny, one so true, yes, I love you.

Verse 5

```
Gm      B♭7                        E♭maj7                Am7(♭5)  D7
Sunny,     yesterday all my life was filled with rain.
Gm      B♭7                             E♭maj7                  Am7(♭5)  D7
Sunny,     you smiled at me and really, really eased the pain.
           Gm                             B♭7
Now the dark days are done and the bright days are here,
E♭maj7                    A♭9
My sunny one shines so sincere,
Am7(♭5)         D7          Gm     Am7(♭5)  D7
Sunny, one so true, I love you.
```

Outro

```
   (D7)    Gm           Am7(♭5)  D7
||: I love you. (Sunny)              :||  Repeat and fade
```

Summer Breeze

Words & Music by Darrell Crofts & Jimmy Seals

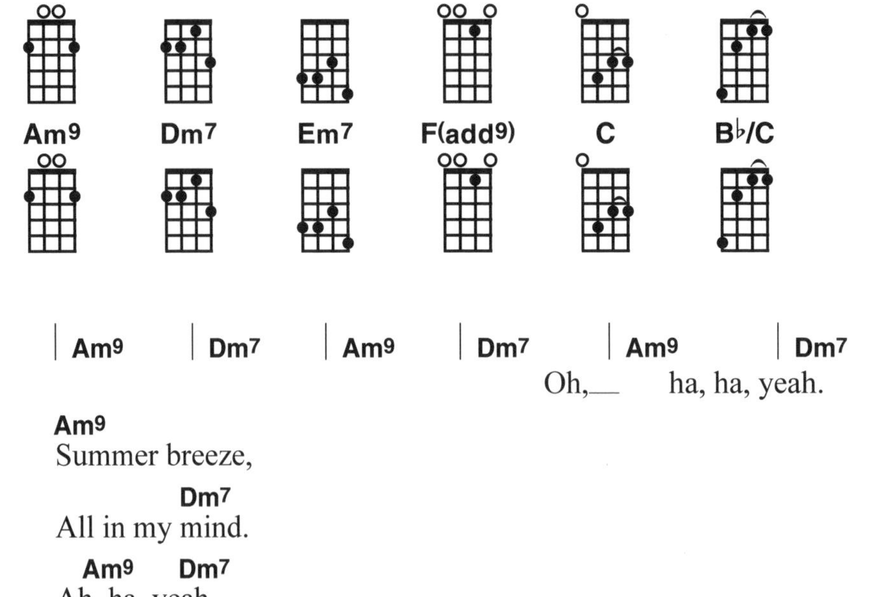

Intro | Am9 | Dm7 | Am9 | Dm7 | Am9 | Dm7 |

Oh,__ ha, ha, yeah.

Am9
Summer breeze,

Dm7
All in my mind.

Am9 Dm7
Ah, ha, yeah,

Am9
Summer breeze,

Dm7
All in my mind.

𝄆 Am9 Dm7 | Am9 Dm7 | Am9 | Dm7 𝄇

No, no, no,no, It's all in my mind.

Chorus 1

Dm7 Em7
Summer breeze makes me feel fine

Dm7 F(add9) C
Blowing through the jasmine in my mind.

B♭/C Dm7 Em7
Oh, summer breeze makes me feel fine

Dm7 F(add9) C
Blowing through the jasmine in my mind.

Bm7 E9
All in my mind.

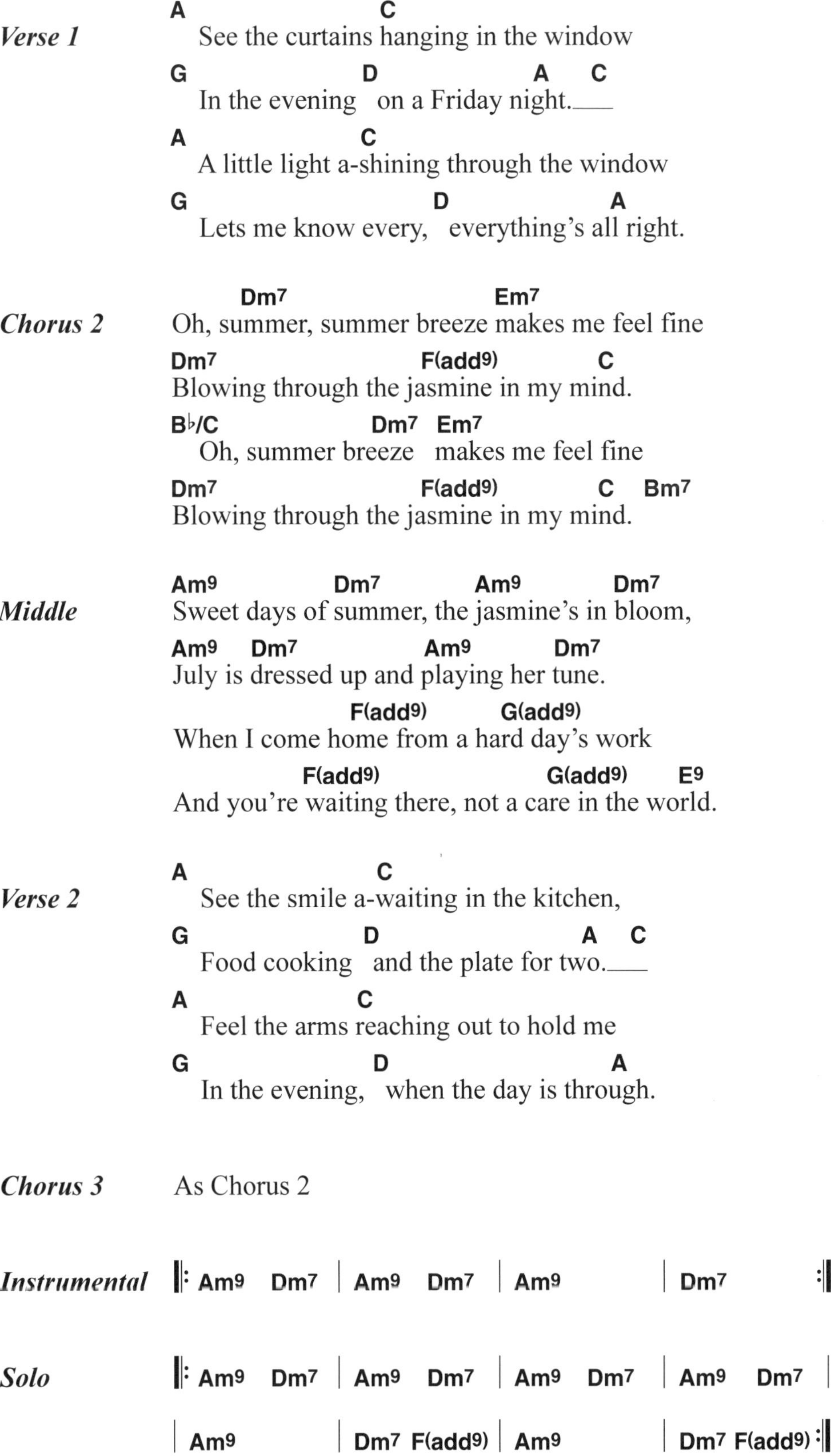

Verse 1

A C
See the curtains hanging in the window
G D A C
In the evening on a Friday night.___
A C
A little light a-shining through the window
G D A
Lets me know every, everything's all right.

Chorus 2

Dm7 Em7
Oh, summer, summer breeze makes me feel fine
Dm7 F(add9) C
Blowing through the jasmine in my mind.
B♭/C Dm7 Em7
Oh, summer breeze makes me feel fine
Dm7 F(add9) C Bm7
Blowing through the jasmine in my mind.

Middle

Am9 Dm7 Am9 Dm7
Sweet days of summer, the jasmine's in bloom,
Am9 Dm7 Am9 Dm7
July is dressed up and playing her tune.
F(add9) G(add9)
When I come home from a hard day's work
F(add9) G(add9) E9
And you're waiting there, not a care in the world.

Verse 2

A C
See the smile a-waiting in the kitchen,
G D A C
Food cooking and the plate for two.___
A C
Feel the arms reaching out to hold me
G D A
In the evening, when the day is through.

Chorus 3 As Chorus 2

Instrumental 𝄆 Am9 Dm7 | Am9 Dm7 | Am9 | Dm7 𝄇

Solo 𝄆 Am9 Dm7 | Am9 Dm7 | Am9 Dm7 | Am9 Dm7 |
| Am9 | Dm7 F(add9) | Am9 | Dm7 F(add9) 𝄇

Repeat to fade

Super Freak

Words & Music by Alonzo Miller & Rick James

D7sus2 Am G F Asus4 Esus4

Intro |: D7sus2 Am | G Am | D7sus2 Am | G Am :|

Verse 1
(Am) D7sus2 Am G Am
She's a very kinky girl,
D7sus2 Am G Am
The kind you don't take home to mother.
D7sus2 Am G Am
She will never let your spirits down___
D7sus2 Am G Am
Once you get her off the street, oh girl.

Verse 2
(Am) D7sus2 Am G Am
She likes the boys in the band,
D7sus2 Am G Am
She says that I'm her all-time favourite.
D7sus2 Am G Am
When I make my move to her room it's the right time,
D7sus2 Am G Am
She's never hard to please, oh no.

Chorus 1
D7sus2 Am F Am
That girl is pretty wild now, (the girl's a super freak)
D7sus2 Am F Am
The kind of girl you read about (in new-wave maga - zines).
D7sus2 Am F Am
That girl is pretty kinky, (the girl's a super freak)
D7sus2 Am F Am
I really love to taste her (every time we meet).
F G Am F G Am
She's all right, she's all right,
F G Am Asus4
That girl's all right___ with me,
F Esus4
Yeah, hey, hey, hey, hey.

Bridge 1

| D7sus2 Am | G Am |

```
         D7sus2       Am
She's a super freak,     super freak
G                 Am     D7sus2  Am
   She's super - freaky, yow.
G               Am
   Everybody sing,
D7sus2       Am        G      Am
Super freak,     super freak.
```

Verse 3

```
(Am)    D7sus2        Am        G                   Am
She's a very special girl, (the kind of girl you want to know)
                D7sus2            Am       G            Am
From her head down to her toenails, (down to her feet, yeah)
                D7sus2            Am              G             Am
And she'll wait for me at backstage with her girlfriends
D7sus2        Am    G              Am
In a limou - sine (going back in Chinatown).
```

Verse 4

```
(Am)                D7sus2  Am                  G       Am
Three's not a crowd to her, she says, (me - nage a trois)
                       D7sus2          Am     G  Am
Room seven - fourteen, I'll be waiting.
             D7sus2              Am                  G       Am
When I get there she's got incense, wine and candles,
     D7sus2         Am     G Am
It's such a freaky scene.
```

Chorus 2

```
          D7sus2      Am        F             Am
That girl is pretty kinky, (the girl's a super freak)
         D7sus2          Am          F                 Am
The kind of girl you read about (in new-wave maga - zines).
          D7sus2      Am           F         Am
That girl is pretty wild now, (the girl's a super freak)
   D7sus2         Am       F              Am
I really like to taste her (every time we meet).
F     G  Am   F    G  Am
She's all right, she's all right,
          F   G  Am     Asus4
That girl's all  right______ with me,
F     Esus4
Yeah,        hey, hey, hey, hey.
```

Bridge 2 | D7sus2 Am | G Am |

```
            D7sus2       Am
She's a super freak,     super freak
G                    Am     D7sus2  Am
   She's super - freaky, yow.
G           Am
   Temp - tations sing,
D7sus2  Am      G        Am
(Oh, oh, oh, oh, oh, oh, oh.)
D7sus2       Am
Super freak,     super freak
G                  Am
   That girl's a super freak
D7sus2  Am      G        Am
(Oh, oh, oh, oh, oh, oh, oh.).
```

Verse 5

```
(Am)    D7sus2      Am    G  Am
She's a very kinky girl,
                D7sus2              Am      G  Am
The kind you won't take home to mother.
              D7sus2          Am           G  Am
She will never let your spirits down___
               D7sus2         Am
Once you get her off the street.
G  Am
   Blow, Daddy!
```

Outro sax solo |: D7sus2 Am | F Am | D7sus2 Am | F Am :| *Repeat to fade*

Teardrops

Words & Music by Linda Womack & Cecil Womack

Fmaj7 Dm7 G Am7 C Em7 G6

To match original recording, tune ukulele down one semitone

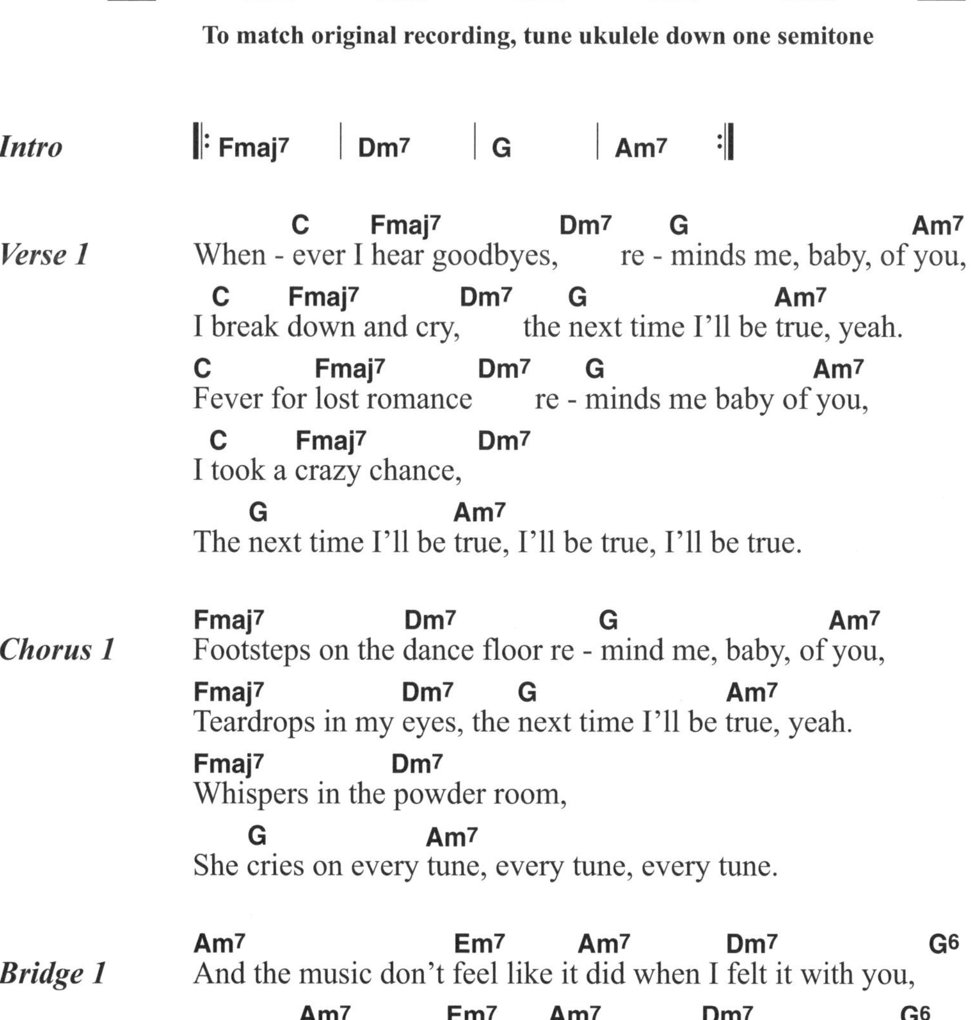

Intro |: Fmaj7 | Dm7 | G | Am7 :|

Verse 1

C Fmaj7 Dm7 G Am7
When - ever I hear goodbyes, re - minds me, baby, of you,

C Fmaj7 Dm7 G Am7
I break down and cry, the next time I'll be true, yeah.

C Fmaj7 Dm7 G Am7
Fever for lost romance re - minds me baby of you,

C Fmaj7 Dm7
I took a crazy chance,

G Am7
The next time I'll be true, I'll be true, I'll be true.

Chorus 1

Fmaj7 Dm7 G Am7
Footsteps on the dance floor re - mind me, baby, of you,

Fmaj7 Dm7 G Am7
Teardrops in my eyes, the next time I'll be true, yeah.

Fmaj7 Dm7
Whispers in the powder room,

G Am7
She cries on every tune, every tune, every tune.

Bridge 1

Am7 Em7 Am7 Dm7 G6
And the music don't feel like it did when I felt it with you,

Am7 Em7 Am7 Dm7 G6
Nothing that I do or feel ever feels like I felt it with you.

```
Instrumental 1 ||: Fmaj7 | Dm7 | G | Am7 :||

          (Am7)      Fmaj7             Dm7    G                  Am7
Verse 2   When I'm dancing 'round,      re - minds me, baby, of you,
                   Fmaj7          Dm7    G                Am7
          I really let you down,      the next time I'll be true, yeah.
                   Fmaj7          Dm7
          I took a crazy chance,
              G             Am7
          She cries on every tune, every tune, every tune.


Chorus 2  As Chorus 1


Bridge 2  As Bridge 1


Instrumental 2 As Instrumental 1

          (Am7)    Fmaj7         Dm7    G             Am7
Verse 3   Hurting deep inside,      she cries on every tune,
                   Fmaj7          Dm7
          I break down and cry,
              G             Am7
          She cries on every tune, every tune, every tune.


Chorus 3  As Chorus 1

          Am7                   Em7      Am7        Dm7              G6
Bridge 3  And the music don't feel like it did when I felt it with you.
                  Am7         Em7     Am7          Dm7              G6
          Nothing that I do or feel ever feels like I felt it with you.
                  Am7           Em7      Am7        Dm7              G6
          And the music don't feel like it did when I felt it with you.
                  Am7         Em7     Am7          Dm7              G6
          Nothing that I do or feel ever feels like I felt it with you.

          Oh-oh, oh-oh, oh-oh, oh-oh-oh-oh.
```

Instrumental 3 ||: Fmaj7 | Dm7 | G | Am7 :||

```
              (Am7)     Fmaj7          Dm7  G  Am7
Outro         Fever for lost romance.
                      Fmaj7          Dm7  G  Am7
              I took a crazy chance.
                     Fmaj7            Dm7     G                      Am7
              Lovers holding hands       re - minds me, baby, of you.
              Fmaj7  Dm7    G                   Am7
                            Next time I'll be true.    Fade out
```

Theme From 'Shaft'

Words & Music by Isaac Hayes

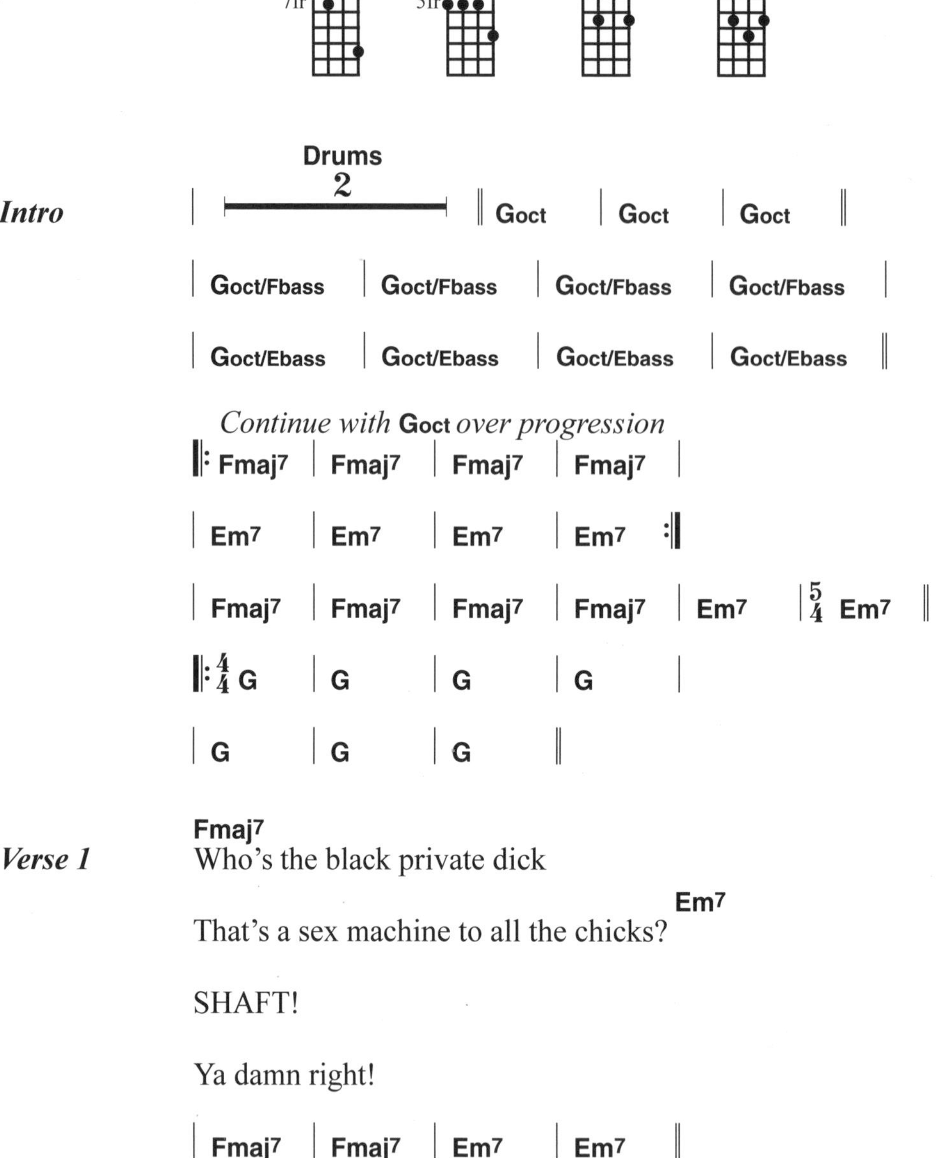

Verse 2

Fmaj7
Who is the man that would risk his neck

Em7
For his brother man?

SHAFT!

Can you dig it?

| Fmaj7 | Fmaj7 | Em7 | Em7 ||

Verse 3

Fmaj7
Who's the cat that won't cop out

When there's danger all about?

Em7
SHAFT!

Right On!

Verse 4

Fmaj7
They say this cat Shaft is a bad mother

SHUT YOUR MOUTH!

Em7
I'm talkin' 'bout Shaft.

Then we can dig it!

Verse 5

Fmaj7
He's a complicated man

Em7
But no one understands him but his woman

JOHN SHAFT!

Outro

| 7/4 G | G ||

| 4/4 Fmaj7 | Fmaj7 | G[illegible] | G[illegible] |

| Fmaj7 | Fmaj7 | Em7 | Em7 | Fmaj7 ||

We Are Family

Words & Music by Bernard Edwards & Nile Rodgers

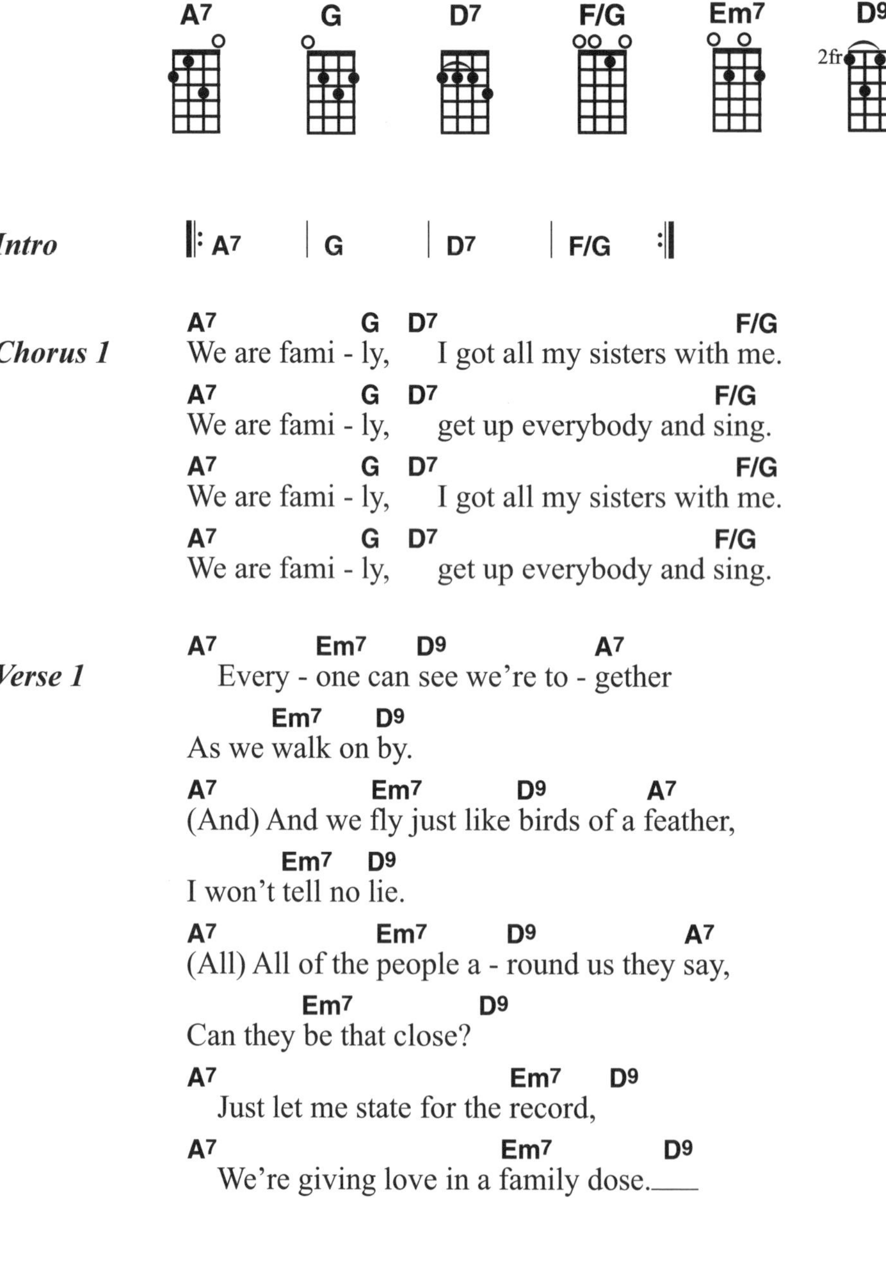

Intro ‖: A7 | G | D7 | F/G :‖

Chorus 1

```
A7               G   D7                        F/G
We are fami - ly,    I got all my sisters with me.
A7               G   D7                      F/G
We are fami - ly,    get up everybody and sing.
A7               G   D7                        F/G
We are fami - ly,    I got all my sisters with me.
A7               G   D7                      F/G
We are fami - ly,    get up everybody and sing.
```

Verse 1

```
A7           Em7       D9              A7
   Every - one can see we're to - gether
        Em7      D9
As we walk on by.
A7                   Em7          D9          A7
(And) And we fly just like birds of a feather,
         Em7   D9
I won't tell no lie.
A7                  Em7          D9              A7
(All) All of the people a - round us they say,
           Em7                D9
Can they be that close?
A7                              Em7       D9
   Just let me state for the record,
A7                             Em7              D9
   We're giving love in a family dose.___
```

Chorus 2 As Chorus 1

Verse 2

A7   Em7   D9   A7
Living life is fun and we've just begun   to get our share

Em7   D9
Of this world's de - lights.

A7   Em7   D9   A7
(High) High hopes we have   for the fu - ture

Em7   D9
And our goal's in sight.

A7   Em7
(We) No, we don't get de - pressed,

D9   A7   Em7   D9
Here's what we call our golden rule.

A7   Em7
Have faith in you and the things you do,

D9   A7   Em7   D9
You won't go wrong, oh no, this is our family jewel.___

Chorus 3

As Chorus 1 *Repeat ad lib. to fade*

1 2 3 4 5 6 7 8 9